Bankside

Excavations at
Benbow House
Southwark
London SE1

Anthony Mackinder and Simon Blatherwick

MoLAS ARCHAEOLOGY STUDIES SERIES 3

MUSEUM OF LONDON ARCHAEOLOGY SERVICE

MoLAS ARCHAEOLOGY STUDIES SERIES

1 A 14th-century pottery site in Kingston upon Thames,
Surrey: Excavations at 70–76 Eden Street, Pat Miller & Roy
Stephenson
ISBN 1-901992 07 1

2 Excavations at 72–75 Cheapside/83–93 Queen Street, City of
London, Julian Hill & Aidan Woodger
ISBN 1-901992 08 X

3 Bankside: Excavations at Benbow House, Southwark, London
SE1, Anthony Mackinder & Simon Blatherwick
ISBN 1-901992.12.8

Published by the Museum of London Archaeology Service
Copyright © Museum of London 2000

Designed by Tracy Wellman, MoLAS
Typeset and layout by Jeannette van der Post, MoLAS
Edited by Monica Kendall
Reprographics by Andy Chopping, MoLAS

Printed by the Lavenham Press,
Lavenham, Suffolk CO10 9RN

CONTRIBUTORS

Principal authors	Anthony Mackinder, Simon Blatherwick
Pottery	Roy Stephenson
Small finds and glass	Geoff Egan
Ceramic building material	Terence Paul Smith
Animal remains	Jane Liddle
Molluscs	Lisa Gray-Rees, Alan Pipe
Botanical remains	Lisa Gray-Rees
Illustrations	Sarah Jones, Jane Sandoe, Kikar Singh
Photography	Edwin Baker, Andy Chopping, Margaret Cox, Liv Gröenli
Project management	Robin Densem, Gillian King, Peter Rowsome, Derek Seeley, Tracy Wellman
Academic adviser	Stephen Humphrey
Editing	Monica Kendall, Peter Rowsome
French & German summaries	Agnès Shepherd, Frederieke Hammer

CONTENTS

FIGURES

TABLES

ABSTRACT

This report presents the results of evaluation and excavation work at Benbow House, Bankside, Southwark between 1995 and 1999 (TQ 3223 8051) (MoL site code BAN95).

The site lies next to the Thames, but some way from the Borough High Street area which was the main focus of activity in the Roman and medieval periods. A peat deposit, dated to the Bronze Age, and other waterlain deposits show that the land was subject to the rise and fall of the Thames over a considerable period (OA1). The earliest extant evidence of human activity within the excavation area was an attempt at land consolidation in the 12th or 13th century (OA2). This external activity was followed by three periods of building dating from the 13th century onwards. A thick, site-wide deposit of crushed chalk was used to stabilise the land prior to the construction of buildings (OA3). A total of nine or 10 buildings can be dated to the 13th and 14th centuries (B1–B10). The buildings had chalk walls and probably included the remains of the 'stews' – inns or brothels known from documentary sources as The Bell & Cock and The Unicorn. A dump of Surrey Whiteware pottery was recovered from a feature in an external area to the south of Buildings 5 and 9 (OA9).

Further buildings were constructed on the site in the 16th and 17th centuries and included a possible second phase to Building 2. To the west another building was interpreted as a possible kennel (B11). External activity towards the south-east corner of the site (OA12) was followed by the construction of what appeared to be a large, multi-sided building (B12),
perhaps the animal-baiting arena known from documentary and cartographic evidence. A large quantity of horse and dog bones were recovered from deposits associated with Building 12 (OA13). Evidence of the butchery of predominantly old horses may suggest that these animals were being fed to the dogs kept nearby for animal-baiting. To the north of Building 12, a dump of tin-glazed pottery (delftware) recovered from a reused medieval cellar (B13) provided the first excavated evidence of the Bear Gardens pothouse that was in operation from 1702 to 1710. Other dumps excavated in external areas (OA5–OA8 and OA10–OA11) contained important glass and glassworking debris, probably from a nearby glasshouse that began c 1671 and had possibly ceased operation by 1748.

The final phase of the excavated evidence included the remains of 18th- and 19th-century brick buildings (B14–B29) reflecting the later use of the site as a foundry and metalworks owned by the Bradley family and later James Benbow. These buildings were not fully excavated, and although the remains of a furnace were found, they are thought mainly to have had ancillary functions. Metalworking debris included numerous examples of buckles. External areas between buildings B20 and B25 (OA14) and to the east of buildings B14–B16 (OA15) were the subject of some excavation and revealed evidence of industrial drains.

The Benbow House excavation is an example of the recent trend towards the preservation of archaeological remains in situ, with excavation only in those areas where archaeological deposits would be subject to unavoidable and total destruction during redevelopment. The adoption of this approach at Benbow House resulted in only partial investigation of the presumed animal-baiting arena and the 18th- and 19th-century brick buildings. These structures have been preserved where they were present, below 3.70m OD, the lowest level of destruction caused by the new building's concrete slab. Elsewhere on the site the new car park basement and pile cap positions entailed the removal of all the archaeological deposits, and that is where the archaeological work was concentrated.

ACKNOWLEDGEMENTS

MoLAS would like to thank Chelsfield Plc for their generous funding of the excavations at Benbow House and their continuing support during the post-excavation analysis and the production of this publication. Particular thanks go to Nick Roberts of Chelsfield. Thanks also go to Steve Bouchard and Ken Murphy of Berkely Homes, and Tom Fitzpatrick and Ali Arabacci of Watermans.

We would also like to thank the London Borough of Southwark's Senior Archaeology Officer John Dillon, and later Sarah Gibson, for their input and support of this project.

The MoLAS field team who worked on the site were Portia Askew, Bruno Barber, Penny Bruce, Howard Burkhill, Carrie Cowan, Lesley Dunwoodie, Peter Durnford, Kieron Heard, Richard Hewett, Julian Hill, Simon Hinder, Elizabeth Howe, John Minkin, Jayne Pilkington, Dave Saxby (who supervised the evaluation phase), Richard Turnbull, Aidan Woodger and Robin Wroe-Brown. The site survey work was undertaken by Duncan Lees, Kate Pollard and Marek Ziebart, while Margaret Cox provided the site photography. Over the years many others have also been involved with aspects of the on-site investigations and apologies are extended to anyone we have omitted.

The archaeological project has been managed by Gillian King, Robin Densem and Derek Seeley, successively. Peter Rowsome has provided post-excavation project management and editorial advice. The authors would also like to thank Stephen Humphrey, who acted as academic adviser to the project and provided valuable advice on the final publication draft.

Geoff Egan would like to thank John Shepherd: the section on glass owes much to his expertise, which was generously available during its compilation. Other specialists involved in the project, but not listed as contributors, include Charlotte Ainsley, who completed a preliminary assessment of the animal bones.

The authors would also like to thank the staffs of the British Library, the Greater London Sites and Monuments Record, the Guildhall Library Maps and Manuscripts Department, the London Metropolitan Archives, the Public Record Office and the Southwark Local Studies Library for their help.

1

Introduction

1.1 Location and circumstances of fieldwork

This publication reports on the archaeological evaluations and excavations conducted at Benbow House in the London Borough of Southwark (Museum of London archaeological site code BAN95). The site (Ordnance Survey national grid reference TQ 3223 8051) is located on the south bank of the River Thames and is bounded by Bankside to the north, Bear Gardens to the east, New Globe Walk (formerly Emerson Street) to the west, and 20–22 New Globe Walk to the south (Figs 1 and 2). The site lies within the Bear Gardens Conservation Area and the Borough, Bermondsey and Riverside Archaeological Priority Zone (Southwark 1995).

The need for archaeological work was brought about by a planning application for the demolition of the 1950s' Benbow House and the construction of a new residential building with deep basements for car parking. Preliminary documentary research (Blatherwick & Densem 1994) had identified the site as the location of medieval tenement properties and possibly the location of two animal-baiting arenas. Although it was assumed previous buildings would have disturbed the site's archaeological deposits it was necessary to conduct on-site investigations to assess the survival of any remains. Archaeology is now, as a result of Planning Policy Guidance 16 (PPG 16 1990), a material consideration in the granting of planning consent. PPG 16 provides planning authorities with a staged approach to the consideration of archaeological remains that may survive on a development site and states that where there are 'nationally important archaeological remains ... that are affected by a proposed development there should be a presumption in favour of their physical preservation' (1990, A8).

The Museum of London Archaeology Service (MoLAS) carried out an initial archaeological evaluation in 1995. This comprised three evaluation trenches, E1, E2 and E3 (see Fig 2), located in the car park area to the east of Benbow House. Medieval and post-medieval archaeological deposits, including the possible remains of an animal-baiting arena, were identified (Saxby 1996, 44). These findings resulted in an excavation strategy being developed, by English Heritage and the London Borough of Southwark, which would preserve identified archaeological remains where possible and excavate those threatened by the new development.

The first phase of excavation took place, from July to September 1997, in the car park area to the east of Benbow House prior to demolition (Excavation Trenches 1 to 5 inclusive). Excavation involved the reduction of the ground surface by controlled use of machine down to a level of 3.25m OD. Archaeological deposits and features identified above this level were digitally recorded by Penmap for Windows. The deposits exposed in the southern half of the site were then preserved *in situ* by laying a covering of inert Buckland sand, sealed by a layer of crushed concrete, to a level of 3.70m OD, this being the base of potential disturbance caused by the new development.

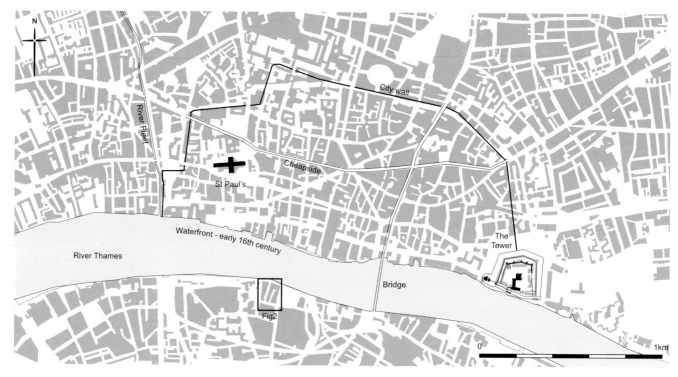

Fig 1 Site location 1:20,000. © Crown copyright. All rights reserved. Corporation of London LA 087254 00/03

As the proposed new pile layout would be using the same positions as previous foundations that had already removed all the archaeological deposits, there was no further disturbance to the archaeology in this area of the site. This preservation methodology included the area containing the structure recorded in the evaluation and thought to be an animal-baiting arena.

As the northern half of the site would be disturbed by the proposed new pile layout there would be destruction of archaeological deposits in certain areas. This allowed the excavation of Trenches 1, 2 and 3, whose locations were dictated by the positions of the new piles. Following completion of the excavations the trenches were backfilled and the northern half of the site was covered with sand and then a layer of crushed concrete up to a level of 3.70m OD. Information from the excavations in this area of the site resulted in a slight change in the piling layout, to allow for the preservation of several walls.

During the demolition of Benbow House concrete pile caps belonging to an earlier building were removed in the north-west corner of the site. This was monitored as part of a watching brief and although the area was heavily disturbed some archaeology had survived.

Following demolition a second phase of excavation took place. This was also in the car park area, with Trench 4 and five pile locations (Piles 8 to 12) excavated in December 1997. Four of the pile holes were located adjacent to Bear Gardens and the fifth was located at the west end of Trench 3. After excavation all were backfilled with spoil and a layer of crushed concrete up to a level of 3.70m OD. Excavation of Trench 5 took place in January 1998 and found archaeological deposits had survived below the now demolished Benbow House.

This resulted in a further watching brief being conducted, during the summer of 1999, to monitor the bulk excavation of the car park basements beneath the new development.

1.2 Geology and topography

The underlying topography of the Bankside area is that of alluvially deposited clays and sand and gravel islands (eyots) on which the early settlement of Southwark was located. Areas of high, natural sand and gravel are interspersed by large, glacially formed and alluvially filled channels with north Southwark having been subject to land reclamation from the Roman period onwards. This land reclamation, with interspersed periods of riverine inundation, led to a build-up of deposits that are of importance in understanding the later development of the area.

Evidence for the varying nature of the natural topography comes from archaeological work at sites near Benbow House. At Skinmarket Place (TQ 3217 8043), some 75m to the south-west, part of a natural sand and gravel island was recorded at 0.66m OD, while at Anchor Terrace (TQ 3235 8035), some 200m south-east, natural gravel was recorded at an upper level of −2.60m OD and a lower level of −3.64m OD.

Archaeological interventions have also recorded the presence of a naturally formed layer of peat – possibly Late Bronze Age (c 1000 BC) – within the Bankside area. The peat is thought to have developed during regressions of the Thames. At 5–15 Bankside (TQ 3236 8045) to the east of the site, peat deposits were recorded at between −0.30m OD and −0.60m OD

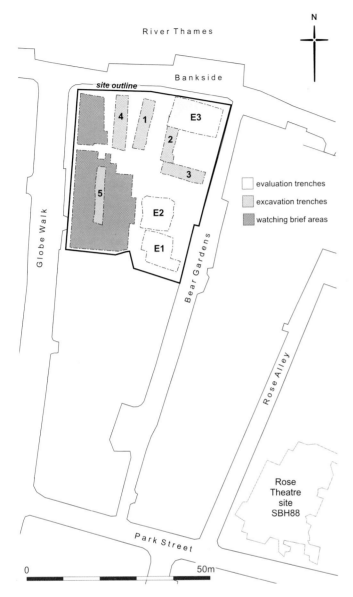

Fig 2 *Areas of archaeological investigation within the site boundaries 1:1000. © Crown copyright. All rights reserved. Corporation of London LA 087254 00/03*

(M G Dennis, pers comm). At Anchor Terrace peat was recorded at −2.04m OD, and at Southbridge House − now known as Rose Court − (TQ 3227 8042) peat, sealed by waterlain clays, was recorded at −0.30m OD.

Subsequent to the peat accumulation, a rise in the level of the Thames appears to have taken place. The available evidence points to a period of high water level in the later prehistoric period. Evidence from 5–15 Bankside and from Southbridge House shows a transition from peat to peaty clays and then to pure clay, suggesting that this rise was a gradual process rather than the result of erosive flooding.

Post-Roman riverine inundation again deposited alluvial clays that were cut by ditches and gullies. The area was, again, the subject of land-reclamation schemes in the medieval period with the bishops of Winchester building embankments in the 12th to 14th centuries (Carlin 1996, 40). It is such a sequence of activity that was recorded at 5–15 Bankside. From the evidence recorded at Skinmarket Place, further inundation

took place in the 14th or 15th century and it appears that large areas, probably on both sides of Borough High Street, remained waterlogged until the 16th or 17th century (Graham 1978, 516).

Cartographic evidence from the mid 16th century onwards shows the area around the site beginning to be developed with roads, alleys and drainage systems (sewers). The sewers were regulated from the 16th century by the Surrey and Kent Commissioners for Sewers whose records provide information concerning property holding on Bankside. That the sewers remained as open ditches until the early 19th century is shown by the records of the Clink Court Leet for 1814 to 1824 (Guildhall Library MS 1513A). Evidence of these sewers has been archaeologically examined, to the east of Benbow House, on the site of the Rose theatre (Bowsher & Blatherwick 1990).

1.3 Archaeological and historical background

Archaeological background

The Bankside area has been the subject of a programme of archaeological investigations (Thompson *et al* 1998) which provide the background to the site.

At 5–15 Bankside excavations revealed a waterlain sequence, probably part of a large creek running inland from the river. The lowest level comprised a thick peat deposit. A dump of mid 14th-century pottery, which included many wasters, may provide evidence of a previously unknown Bankside kiln, producing Surrey Whitewares. The site did not appear to have been built up until relatively late, the sequence being overlaid by the fragmentary remains of 16th- and 17th-century buildings. Further excavations on the same site in 1987 (TQ 3240 8045) revealed flooded and reclaimed marshland, and drainage channels of medieval date. Properties dating to the 14th century and later were recorded with a timber revetment, incorporating planking from a medieval clinker-built boat, located 10m south of the modern riverbank. Further to the north, chalk rubble had been dumped to form the foundations for the 14th-century stone river wall.

Directly to the west at 37–46 Bankside (TQ 3218 8051), now the site of the reconstructed Globe theatre, excavations in 1987 found the tops of at least three 16th-century parallel revetments aligned east–west. These were constructed of reused timber, including parts of Tudor wheelbarrows, and possibly represent fish tanks or ponds.

At nearby Skin Market Place, excavation in 1988–9 located a previously unknown island of high sand which yielded Neolithic pottery and flints sealed by flood deposits and early medieval ditches. These were covered in turn by further flood

3

clays of 14th- to 15th-century date. The excavation also recorded evidence of the King's Pike Garden, in the form of timber-revetted fish ponds.

At Southbridge House remains of the Rose theatre (c 1587–1605) were recorded and at the rear of 27 Bankside (TQ 3226 8048), south-east of Benbow House, remains thought to be part of the Hope playhouse have recently been recorded (Cowan 1999).

Work at the site of the Millennium footbridge (TQ 3205 8054) found a sequence of timber revetments, the earliest activity being 12th century in date (R Wroe-Brown, pers comm).

Documentary and historical background

The documentary study of the site is enhanced by the large number of sources and the fact that the site fell, for a considerable period of its history, under two large property owners. The development of the site and the surrounding area from the 12th century onwards, also provides a reflection of the urban development of Southwark and, more particularly, Bankside. In the course of its history the site has been the location of medieval properties, animal-baiting arenas and early industries. Its proximity to both the river and the heart of Southwark means that the site has been an estate subject to speculation and redevelopment.

The history of the site is inextricably linked with ecclesiastical landlords and the Henrician dissolution of the monasteries in the mid 16th century. The subsequent leasing of land and subdivision of landholdings make exactitude concerning landholdings difficult. Prior to the Dissolution the Benbow House site lay on land in the ownership of the bishop of Winchester and the prioress of Stratford-at-Bow. At the Dissolution the Crown gained control over the prioress's land while the bishops of Winchester appear to have leased or sold their property to existing tenants. However, for ease of understanding, the terms 'Crown land' and 'bishop of Winchester's land' will initially be used (see Fig 5). After the Dissolution the Crown land was leased to Henry Polsted and then to Robert Liveseye and Gerrard Gore. The terms 'Crown land' and 'Polsted lease' and 'Liveseye/Gore lease' will be used to describe the activity on the western side of the site in the 16th and for most of the 17th centuries. The freehold of the Crown land appears to have been sold in 1671–2 as part of Charles II's revenue-raising activity, but the bishop of Winchester's land was held until 1866 when it was sold by the Ecclesiastical Commissioners (Braines 1924, 96).

Immediately after the Dissolution further alterations in ecclesiastical jurisdiction over the land occurred. After the suppression of Southwark Priory in 1539–40, the parish of St Margaret, within which the site was located, amalgamated with the parish of St Mary Magdalen to form the new parish of St Saviour.

The documentary study has involved the use of both published and unpublished sources. Initial use of published sources, particularly the work of W W Braines (1924) and Martha Carlin (1996), provided a large amount of the introductory and background material relating to the site, as well as providing references for some of the primary sources. Information concerning other primary sources was also provided by the bibliography in Jeremy Boulton's 1987 publication.

Searches for primary sources took place in the British Library, London Metropolitan Archives and the Southwark Local Studies Library, Borough High Street. Particularly useful were the St Saviour's Land Tax and Poor Rate Books, held by the London Borough of Southwark, and the records of the churchwardens of St Saviour held in the London Metropolitan Archives (Draper 1952). The records of St Saviour are incredibly detailed and further study of them would undoubtedly provide greater information concerning the occupants of the site, particularly from the 17th century onwards.

1.4 Organisation of this report

This report forms part of the MoLAS Archaeology Studies series. The series is primarily intended to facilitate production of archaeological reports for the London region by working closely in association with local and regional societies. The series aims to present smaller or medium-scale archaeological investigations, sometimes as single-site sequences and at other times with more than one site being linked by broad chronological or subject-matter themes. The series is further designed to link with the MoLAS Monograph series, through consistent use of format and design. MoLAS would welcome any comments on the design and content of this series.

The arrangement of each volume in the Studies series will follow a similar order, where, for each site involved, the circumstances of the investigation(s) precede a chronological narrative (chapter 2) divided where appropriate by archaeological 'period' and land-use entities (buildings, open areas, roads and structures). In the Benbow House publication the main periods of site use begin with a documentary account followed by the archaeological evidence. A period discussion draws the two types of evidence together. Selected parts of specialist reports on the finds retrieved from the site are integrated within the text where possible, with specialist catalogues and detailed reports forming additional chapters (chapters 3–5) which follow on from the presentation of the sequence. Expansion codes for the pottery forms, fabrics and decoration can be found in the Appendix. The date ranges in Tables 1–4 are based on fabric date ranges, forms, relative number of sherds and condition of sherds. As the site is closely linked with the history of animal-baiting in Southwark a glossary of terms used in the documentary accounts is provided at the end of the book.

1.5 Textual and graphic conventions in this report

The basic unit of cross-reference throughout the archive that supports this report is the context number. This is a unique number given to each archaeological event on site (such as a layer, wall, pit cut, road surface etc). Context numbers in the text are normally shown thus: [100].

The archaeological sequence is expressed in terms of periods and land use. The periods are unique to the evidence from the site, and are based on a combination of artefactual dating and major stratigraphic development of the site. A particular period may be subdivided into phases.

This report employs the same Building and Open Area numbers as are used in the archive report (sometimes here abbreviated B and OA). These features are numbered sequentially through the excavated sequence, from the bottom up, and describe the history of the land use recorded on the site. Given the relative simplicity of the sequence, a land-use diagram has not been included. The land-use text and accompanying drawings showing development over time are of course an interpretation of the findings as excavated and do not necessarily describe the complete, original structural history of the site or the only 'right' way of presenting it.

Accession numbers given to certain artefacts from the site are shown thus: <100>.

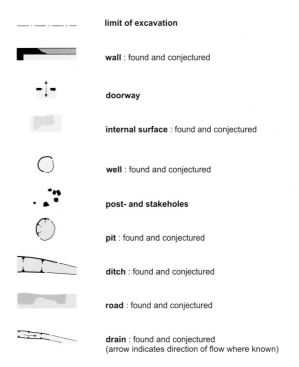

	limit of excavation
	wall : found and conjectured
	doorway
	internal surface : found and conjectured
	well : found and conjectured
	post- and stakeholes
	pit : found and conjectured
	ditch : found and conjectured
	road : found and conjectured
	drain : found and conjectured (arrow indicates direction of flow where known)

Fig 3 Graphic conventions used in this report

The graphic conventions used on the period plans in this report are shown in Fig 3.

2

The archaeological sequence

2.1 Period 1: natural deposits

Open Area 1: natural

The nature of the natural deposits recorded at Benbow House reflected the proximity of the site to the Thames. Monitoring of the bulk excavation for the new car park basements in the watching brief area allowed a great depth of deposits to be examined, and a waterlain blue-grey clay with lenses of finer sand and fragments of twigs was observed at −2.0m OD.

This clay was overlain at c −0.50m OD by a fibrous peat deposit c 1.20m thick. This was laid down in the Bronze Age, a sample (Beta −129555) had a radiocarbon date of 1245 BC to 920 BC (2890±50 BP incalibrated). A further peat deposit c 0.45m thick was observed in Pile Hole 8 at 0.60m OD. This may be of a similar age but the presence of fragments of 13th-century pottery suggests this deposit was truncated or had been disturbed. The difference in height suggests the topography is sloping down towards the west.

Although not reached in Trenches 1 and 2, elsewhere the upper sequence of natural waterlain deposits consisted of bands of clays and silts and occasional bands of sand. The heights of these deposits varied from 0.20m OD to 1.90m OD found in Pile Hole 9. The presence of bone and ceramic building material fragments shows the upper parts of this deposit were being disturbed and mixed by river action or flood events. These deposits again suggest the topography was sloping down to the west.

A sample of the waterlain clay was examined and found to contain abundant freshwater molluscan remains. The most abundant species were *Bithynia tentaculata* L, *Pisidium* sp, and *Theodoxus fluviatilis* L. *Bithynia tentaculata* L is common in large bodies of slow-moving, well-oxygenated hard water (calcareous) in lowland rivers, canals, drainage dykes and lakes, rarely in small closed ponds, and usually in association with dense aquatic vegetation and muddy riverbeds (Kerney 1999, 39; Macan 1977, 41; Janus 1982, 61). The pea shells (*Pisidium* sp) are widely distributed throughout the British Isles and, dependent upon species, are present throughout the range of freshwater habitats. *Theodoxus fluviatilis* L is restricted to well-oxygenated calcareous waters but is able to tolerate both slow- and fast-flowing conditions in rivers, canals and the wash zone of lakes. It is also tolerant of brackish water and mild organic pollution (Macan 1977, 41; Kerney 1999, 24). It prefers hard surfaces such as pebbles, rocks and masonry (Janus 1982, 56) and sunken wood and aquatic plants (Ellis 1969, 69).

Present in smaller numbers were *Bithynia leachii* L, *Lymnea peregra* L, *Planorbis contortus* L, *Planorbis planorbis* L and *Valvata piscinalis* L. *Bithynia leachii* L also prefers hard water, in particular slow, thickly weeded waters (Janus 1982, 61) with high species diversity (Kerney 1999, 40). *Lymnea peregra* L is very common and ubiquitous throughout the British Isles. It is capable of adapting to changing environments and can tolerate mild pollution and seasonal desiccation (Ellis 1969,

104–5, 110). *Planorbis contortus* is a common snail of soft and hard water (Macan 1977, 43) and is able to tolerate a wide range of conditions except seasonal desiccation (Kerney 1999, 63). *Planorbis planorbis* L is common in all kinds of well-vegetated lowland freshwater habitats. It prefers hard water and is able to tolerate seasonal desiccation (Kerney 1999, 58). *Valvata piscinalis* L is common in larger bodies of slowly flowing or still water; it has a preference for muddy or silty substrates, and some tolerance for soft water (Macan 1977, 44; Janus 1982, 58; Kerney 1999, 29).

Period discussion

Archaeological and environmental evidence from this period indicates that the site is located away from the high sand and gravel islands (eyots) within an area of riverine channel fill. The presence of thick bands of peat on top of alluvial clay indicates that the site had been subject to innundation by the Thames followed by the lowering of the water levels, thus allowing the peat to develop. The molluscan assemblage is dominated numerically by *T fluviatilis* and *Bithynia* spp (including *B tentaculata*); both these species are able to tolerate a range of conditions but are abundant in well-oxygenated, slow-moving, calcareous, lowland freshwater bodies with predominantly soft substrates. Although *T fluviatilis* and *L peregra* can both tolerate mild organic pollution, there are no definite indications that either fauna derives from polluted conditions.

2.2 Period 2: 12th- to 13th-century consolidation dumps

Documentary evidence (10th–13th centuries)

Southwark first appears by name in the Burghal Hidage (a list of fortified places) in the early 10th century. King Alfred had probably fortified Southwark at the same time he fortified the city in 886. Possibly a Mercian king had done likewise in the mid 9th century (Carlin 1996, 12). Otherwise, Southwark is not described in detail until Domesday Book in 1086, and even that description is incomplete.

Domesday records that in 1086 Odo, bishop of Bayeux and William I's half-brother, had a minster and tidal waterway which had previously been held by King Edward. Edward received 'two parts of the income from the waterway where the ships moored [and] Earl Godwin the third part', with the men of Southwark testifying 'that before 1066 no one but the King took toll on the shore or on the waterfront' (Morris 1975, 5.28). Domesday also records that the bishop 'gave the church and the waterway first to Aethelwold and then to Ralph, in exchange for a house'. The shore and waterfront are described in Domesday as 'strande' and 'vico Aquae', with *vico* (or *vicus*) apparently meaning a small town or urban district (Morris 1975, 5.28).

The extent of the 11th-century *vicus* is not certain although it appears to have been completely destroyed in 1066 when a force of 500 of William's knights 'burnt all the buildings on the south bank after a sortie against the Normans from London' (Carlin 1996, 15). It is unlikely to have extended as far west as the Benbow House site. Archaeological and topographical evidence indicates that the site was on alluvial deposits subject to regular inundation by the Thames.

Despite William the Conqueror's brutal attentions in 1066, Southwark had become a thriving suburb 20 years later. There was a dock, trading shore, fishery (the manors of Walkinstead and Ditton 'received rents from their Southwark properties in the form of herring renders'), minster and a property market (Carlin 1996, 17–18).

Southwark's development and its proximity to London must have been part of the appeal the location held for the bishop of Winchester when looking for a London property. Bishop Henry of Blois (brother of King Stephen) acquired a manor, c 1144–9, from the monks of Bermondsey for £2 per annum, the estate covering 60 to 70 acres. Flooding, however, appears to have been a serious problem and to combat this the bishop carried out extensive embanking in the 12th and 13th centuries (Carlin 1996, 40).

Archaeological evidence

Open Area 2

In the south-west corner of the main watching brief area beneath Benbow House, a number of stakes and horizontally laid wattling were observed. These were undated but may have been an attempt at consolidation of the waterlain deposits. In Trenches 1 and 5 (see Fig 2) some of the waterlain deposits contained fragments of 12th- and 13th-century pottery and may have been an attempt to raise and consolidate the land surface.

The three main domesticates, cattle, sheep/goat and pig, were represented, with an environmental sample from context [99] containing a small number of bird and fish bones. A chicken distal humerus and thornback ray (*Raja clavata*) dermal denticle were the only identifiable remains from the sample. The thornback ray is common on the Essex coast and would have been caught to eat. Although it is not caught in the Thames estuary today (Wheeler 1979, 170), during the Tudor period the thornback ray may have come further up the lower tidal Thames and been caught in the estuary. Due to the small amount of animal remains from this period, no substantial faunal evidence can be gained.

The sample contained a molluscan assemblage almost identical to a sample from Open Area 1; it differed only in individual count and the presence of oyster shell, barnacle and *Sphaerium* sp, another freshwater bivalve species. The orb mussels, *Sphaerium* spp, are widely distributed throughout the British Isles and are able to exploit a wide range of habitats dependent upon species. Some species are tolerant of organic pollution and of desiccation.

Table 1 Period 2 dating evidence (12th and 13th centuries)

Open Area 2: consolidation dumps				
activity	context	evidence	pot type	date range
Dump	577	Ceramics	KING: CP	1230–1300
			LOND: JUG, JUG APDD,	
			JUG INCW	
			SHER: CP	
			SSW: -	
Dump	692	Ceramics	KING: DJ, JUG RDS, JUG	1230–1400
			STMP, MBOX	

The assemblages within Period 2 produced small groups of typical 12th- and 13th-century pottery such as South Hertfordshire Greyware (SHER). London-type wares (LOND and LCOAR) and the products of the Surrey Whiteware including Kingston ware (KING) and Coarse Border ware (CBW). Notable among the products are a Kingston ware money box and a fragment from a Kingston ware jug decorated with what appears to be an inverted heraldic device consisting of dots over a grid <P1> (see Fig 10).

Period discussion

(Table 1)

The absence of structural archaeological features relating to this period correlates with the documentary evidence of this part of Southwark. It would seem that the main activities within the vicinity of Benbow House were related to land reclamation and control of the River Thames. This activity may well be represented by the survival of timber wattling and stakes although it is possible that these features could also be connected with fishing or the storage of live fish. The molluscan fauna infers that there were similar depositional conditions as found in Period 1.

2.3 Period 3: 13th- to 15th-century development

Documentary evidence

There appears to be little evidence of occupational development on Bankside before the 13th century. Martha Carlin (1996, 40) suggests that the street called Bankside can probably be identified with a causeway made in 1218–19 and postulates that the causeway ran between the manor mill at Bank End, east of the site, and a house belonging to R(obert) de Bolonia. Bankside, however, is not mentioned in medieval deeds, which normally refer to properties extending from the river in the north to Maiden Lane (modern-day Park Street) in the south, possibly suggesting that the causeway was a private access road created on top of the riverside embankments. Maiden(s) Lane, to the south of Benbow House, is first recorded as '*wala Puellarum*' (embankment of the girls) in a charter of 1251–66

suggesting that prostitution was already established there (Carlin 1996, 40). The pipe rolls of the bishops of Winchester record fines imposed on girls ('*de puella*') by the bishop's manor court.

The description of the area between Maiden Lane and Bankside as the Stews appears to originate in the mid 14th century. Carlin (1996, 49 and n 128) records the pipe roll for 1349/50 describing a tenement as lying '*apud les Stufes*', with 'stew' apparently referring to both fish ponds and brothels, both of which appear on the early maps of Southwark. The term 'stew', meaning fish pond or tank, apparently came into English usage 'from the French *estui*, meaning case, sheath and a tub for keeping fish in a boat' (Carlin 1996, 211 n 12).

The locale was ideal for fishmongers, prostitutes and brothel owners due to its proximity to the river (for transport and access) and the relative immunity from prosecution found within the bishop's manor. That fishmongers made up a percentage of the population in the mid 14th century appears to be borne out by the fact that of the five property holders presented for not maintaining their ditches at the Stews in 1363, all possessed fish ponds. Four – John Tryg, William Strokelady, William Neuport and Hugh Ware – were fishmongers, with the fifth, William Strode, possibly being a vintner (Carlin 1996, 50 n 129). Brothels and fish ponds were located near the Benbow House site and the name of the second-mentioned individual could indicate that he had more than one occupation on Bankside!

Prostitution was officially sanctioned in Southwark by a City Ordinance of 1393 which ordered the women to keep themselves to Cock Lane in Smithfield and the Stews on Bankside (Carlin 1996, 210; Riley 1868, 535). The City's lack of jurisdiction in the Clink (owned by the bishop of Winchester) had led to it previously attempting to control access to the Stews by banning Thames boatmen from ferrying people there between sunset and sunrise, forbidding them to tie up their boats 'within twenty fathoms of the shore during that time' (Carlin 1996, 213). This contradictory approach was one that the City was also to show in its attitude to stage plays and players, with prostitution, along with large public gatherings, being considered a source of crime.

Despite Bankside's reputation, the number of properties involved in prostitution seems to have been relatively small, rising from seven in 1381 to 18 or so by 1506 (Carlin 1996, 213). The keepers of brothels appear to have been subject to high rents which may have discouraged all but the most committed. In 1481 Thomas Dyconson leased a brothel from the churchwardens of St Margaret's and paid a weekly rent of 3s 8d (£9 3s 4d per annum) whereas other tenants of St Margaret's were paying in the region of 13s 4d per annum (Carlin 1996, 214 n 28).

Although located within the manor of the bishops of Winchester, the stews were privately owned and operated. However, the bishops retained the freehold of two stewhouses, The Bell (also called The Bell & Cock) and The Barge, which were 'leased out to favourite retainers gratis or on easy terms' (Carlin 1996, 213 n 23). To the west

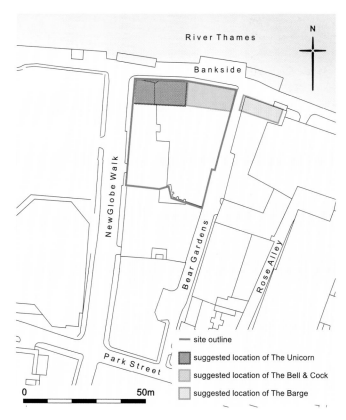

Fig 4 Suggested locations of The Unicorn, The Bell & Cock and The Barge. © Crown copyright. All rights reserved. Corporation of London LA 087254 00/03

of The Bell & Cock and The Barge, on land in the possession of the prioress of Stratford-at-Bow, was a tenement called The Unicorn (Fig 4).

The locations of The Bell & Cock and The Barge appear to be verifiable from a deed of sale dated 17 June 1537 and the records of the transfer of property from the bishop of Winchester to William Payne at the Dissolution. When the property was transferred to Payne, on 6 March 1539/40, it was described as 'certen capytall messauages and tenements called the barge, the bell and the cocke ... being uppon the bancke called the Stewes ... buttinge and lyinge against the Kinges highewaie next the water of Thames on the northe side, and agaynste the tenemente called the rose on the east side, and agaynst the tenemente sometymes the ladie of Stretford on the west side, and agaynst a lane called Mayden lane on the south side' (Braines 1924, 90).

The transfer of property to Payne reveals that The Barge and The Bell & Cock are on the land formerly owned by the bishops of Winchester, while the location of The Barge on the land is ascertained by the details of a sale, dated 17 June 1537, in which William Spence sold his property called The Rose to Henry Polsted. In that sale the tenement and garden sometime called The Rose is described as being 'upon the Stewesbank' with that garden and tenement of Ralph Symonds (the Little Rose Estate on which the Rose theatre was built) to the east and with a tenement called The Barge and the garden that had lately belonged to the prioress of Stratford on the west (Braines 1924, 91; PRO Anc Deed, B.12364). This locates The Barge at the

eastern side of the bishop's land and appears to indicate that The Barge did not extend on to the Benbow House site (see Fig 4). The size of the individual medieval tenements is not known although an indication may be provided by a building contract between Peter Street on one part and Philip Henslowe and Edward Alleyn on the other (see below). In this contract, dated 2 June 1606, Henslowe and Alleyn instruct Street to pull down an existing tenement 'as conteyneth in lengthe from outside to outside fiftye and sixe feete of assize [17.07m], and in bridth from outside to outside sixteene feete [4.88m] of assize' (Collier 1841, 79). Presumably the tenement that Street was instructed to demolish was one of the original medieval buildings on the site (possibly The Bell & Cock). Archaeological evidence may indicate that Street used the foundations of the demolished medieval building for his new construction. It is, of course, dangerous to assume that The Barge would have been the same size as The Bell & Cock and, at present, it is not possible to prove.

To the west of the bishop's land was property which had been owned until the Dissolution by the prioress and nuns of Stratford-at-Bow. At the Dissolution the prioress's land was granted to Ralph Sadler, who sold it in 1538/9 to Henry Polsted, under the description of 'messuages, gardens, lands and tenements ... in the place commonly called the Stewes side formerly ... possessions of the late priory of the nuns of Stratford at Bowe' (Braines 1924, 92). In other descriptions the prioress's property is described as consisting of 12 messuages, 16 gardens and 4 acres of land covered with water (Braines 1924, 92 n).

By this acquisition, Polsted acquired land that enclosed the bishop's land on the east, south and west, including the western part of the Benbow House site. Polsted's ownership of the freehold lasted only until 1552 when the Crown obtained the land (Fig 5), but on 26 April 1552 Polsted was granted a lease of the property for 21 years. Included in the description of this lease was 'the ferm of a capital messuage or inn called "le Unicorn" with garden adjoining' (Braines 1924, 92). Although it is not known exactly where The Unicorn was located, on the Polsted lease it would appear likely (given its status as an inn) that it fronted on to Bankside on the west of the Benbow House site (see Fig 4).

Archaeological evidence

(Fig 6)

Open Area 3

(not illustrated)

The Period 2 external sequence was followed by a major, almost site-wide, phase of consolidation dumping in the form of thick deposits of crushed chalk. The highest level recorded was 2.55m OD in Trench 2 and the lowest was 1.23m OD in Pile Hole 12. The chalk was from 0.60m to 1.0m thick, and in Trench 1 this included a distinct layer of chalk rubble which was not seen in any other area of site. The crushed chalk must originally have been a by-product from an industry such as

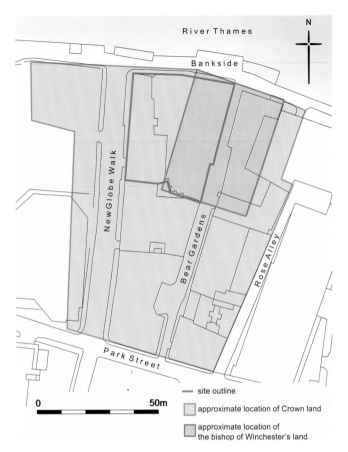

Fig 5 Approximate locations of Crown land and the bishop of Winchester's land. © Crown copyright. All rights reserved. Corporation of London LA 087254 00/03

lime burning for use in building construction. Similar chalk dumps used as consolidation rafts have been noted alongside the river, particularly at Limehouse. Here chalk was brought from Kent and used in limekilns that supplied the City, which are known from 1362/3 (McDonnell 1978, 108). It is probable there were other limekilns located closer to the Benbow House site, that were used in the construction of the nearby Winchester Palace. To the west, on the site of the reconstructed Globe theatre, these chalk dumps were not seen.

No chalk was found in Pile Holes 9 and 10, which may be because this was an area of higher ground and the chalk was being used to fill in lower-lying ground. In the watching brief area there was also a large area where the chalk was not recorded. This may have been the result of later truncation but other than the noticeable lack of chalk, there was no evidence of deliberate activity, such as pit-digging, that could account for this anomaly.

In some areas distinct bands of crushed chalk were noted, occasionally separated by thin bands of grey silt, but in others they appeared to be one single depositional event. Other than some 13th-century pottery recovered from Trench 1 and some intrusive 16th-century pottery, these chalk deposits did not contain inclusions. Their function was to reclaim and consolidate the low-lying marshy land alongside the river to form a stable platform for the construction of buildings. It is probable they were dumped either behind an earth embankment that acted as the river wall or behind a timber revetment that lies outside the areas of investigation.

Open Area 3 produced moderate quantities of both medieval and post-medieval pottery. The medieval includes typically occurring types of the 13th century, including Kingston-type ware and South Hertfordshire Greyware; the latter is more likely to be derived from Limpsfield in Surrey than the South Hertfordshire group of kilns. The later pottery is intrusive and includes a Cistercian-type ware mug decorated with white slip, plus 16th-century redwares.

Building 1

(Fig 6)

The only evidence for Building 1 was found in Evaluation Trench E3 and consisted of two distinct areas of chalk which may have formed footings or an arched foundation for chalk walls. Only the footings of the building survived. The eastern footing was roughly circular at 1.20m in diameter, while the western footing was larger and was possibly square, measuring 2.0m east–west. The technique of using chalk footings for building was only observed in the north-east corner of the site.

Building 2 phase 1

(Fig 6)

Building 2, which was constructed after the western footing of Building 1 was levelled, survived as a length of almost north–south chalk wall and another almost east–west chalk wall. These survivals formed the eastern and southern external walls of a building facing the Thames, with the south wall faced on the outside by flints. The building may have had solid chalk walls or chalk footings supporting a timber-framed wall. The walls were not excavated and their depth is unknown. In common with similar walls elsewhere on the site, it is not thought the walls were built over timber piles, the underlying chalk dump providing sufficient stability. No floor deposits were found in association with Building 2 but the south wall did have a small offset on its inside face at *c* 2.30m OD. As the south wall was truncated, the western limit of the building is unknown, although it does not appear to have continued as far west as the garderobe of Building 7. This would mean that Building 2 was approximately 10m long east–west.

Contexts associated with the primary phase of Building 2 contained small quantities of medieval pottery dating from the 12th–14th centuries, plus some intrusive post-medieval pottery. The primary phase of the building was apparently demolished and sealed by the resulting chalk rubble in the late 15th century, although evidence of a second phase of use or associated structure appears to have continued into Period 4.

Building 3

(Figs 6 and 7)

Building 3 also contained evidence of two phases of use and lay to the west of Buildings 1 and 2, parallel to the river. The first phase of the building apparently lay furthest north and was represented by an east–west aligned chalk wall.

Fig 6 Principal archaeological features, Period 3: 13th and 14th centuries

This wall apparently formed the southern wall of the building, with floor deposits lying to its north in Room A (see Fig 7). The floors were of crushed chalk mixed with silt and charcoal fragments. No east or west returns of the southern wall were found and these must have lain outside the limits of the trench. The alignment of Building 3 varied slightly from Building 2. Pottery associated with Building 3 phase 1 suggests that it dates to the late 13th century.

Outside and to the south of Building 3 phase 1 was the northern edge of a large cut measuring 0.40m deep. The cut was steep-sided and the base sloped gently to the south for over 6.0m. The cut may have been one of the fish ponds known to exist on this part of Bankside from at least the 14th century (Carlin 1996, 49). Fills of clayey silts with crushed chalk and mortar fragments suggest that the feature was enclosed by a masonry lining which was subsequently robbed. Two fragments of Kingston ware pottery gave a date of 13th century to the backfilling.

Deposits sealing the infilled fish pond included part of a 14th-century cobbled surface, laid against the south face of the southern wall of Building 3 phase 1. An east–west wall constructed of chalk, flint, ragstone and greensand fragments was built 3.5m to the south of the earlier wall but was not quite parallel with it. There was no trace of floor deposits in the space between the two walls (Room B), and it is possible that the new wall enclosed an external cobbled area associated with a secondary phase of use of Building 3.

The majority of pottery recovered from Building 3 is medieval, although there was some contamination from later post-medieval wares. The medieval pottery was mostly Surrey Whitewares. The range includes Coarse Border, Kingston, Tudor Green wares and Cheam Whiteware; noteworthy among the forms are a possible Kingston finial fragment, and money boxes in both Kingston and Coarse Border wares. The presence of money box fragments is significant as money boxes are a commonly occurring form in Southwark. The Rose theatre excavations (Bowsher 1998; Bowsher & Blatherwick 1990) revealed large quantities of money box fragments, and in addition they were found at nearby Skinmarket Place (Thompson et al 1998, 216). Additionally there is a Kingston ware lid with an external flange, although broken away, which is well glazed both inside and out <P2> (see Fig 10).

Peg tiles, some with glaze and therefore of medieval date, were recovered from Building 3. Some are of early type (late 12th to early 13th century) and must have been reused. Other material associated with this building includes plain glazed 'Flemish' floor tiles of medieval date and medieval Flemish-type bricks, one perhaps deliberately shaped to form a jamb moulding for a doorway, window, or other feature. Its pale colour may have been exploited to imitate real stone, possibly in a stone building.

Fig 7 Building 3 Room A looking south-west, showing chalk wall (with blocked doorway to left), floor deposits and underlying alluvial deposits. In section to left is a possible fish pond below Room B. Scale 0.5m

Building 4

(Fig 6)

Unlike Buildings 1 to 3, Building 4 may have had only a small frontage overlooking the Thames, with its main frontage facing east or west. It is possible that Building 4, which also had two phases of use, was part of a western range to Building 3 or an eastern range to Building 9, although the restricted nature of the investigations prevents any conclusion.

Building 4 phase 1 comprised two east–west chalk walls and originally had at least two rooms. An opening 0.65m wide in the northern of the two walls may have been a doorway between Room A to the north and Room B to the south. The opening was later blocked with ragstone masonry. The floors in both rooms were composed of crushed chalk. In Room B a 0.50m wide masonry and chalk structure had been built against the south face of the dividing wall near the doorway, perhaps forming a buttress to provide additional support to this wall. Traces of a decayed timber floor were recorded within Room B. Occupation deposits from the floors of both rooms were dated to the 13th century.

The second phase of Building 4 comprised an extension to the south to create another room (Room C). Traces of brickearth floors in Room C were dated to the mid 14th century, suggesting that the extension of the building happened after the construction of Building 5 to the south (see below). Room C may now have formed the southern limit of Building 4, although the room was later altered with the insertion of an east–west partition wall 0.20m wide and constructed of chalk, flint and ragstone. A layer of demolition material in Room B was also dated to the mid 14th century and may have formed a make-up for a new floor, perhaps contemporary to the blocking of the doorway between Rooms A and B.

Dating evidence from Building 4 is dominated by Surrey Whitewares, including another money box. Other noteworthy pottery includes a Coarse Border ware dripping dish and a Fine Kingston-type ware puzzle jug. Non-Surrey wares are limited to small quantities of London-type ware and imports include Siegburg Unglazed Stoneware and Smooth Green-glazed Saintonge ware. Some medieval peg tile was found within the building. Other finds include a fragment of a copper vessel [637] <222>, a fragment of a stone mortar [227] <226> and a copper-alloy thimble [564] <215>. Building 4 had certainly fallen out of use by the mid 16th century, when a pit lined with clay was dug through the sequence associated with Room B.

Building 5

(Fig 6)

Building 5 was set back from the river and lay to the south of Building 4, perhaps also facing or fronting on to an alleyway to the west. The east–west aligned north wall of Building 5 was chalk. The north-east corner of the building was recorded in Trench 1 to the east, the foundation infill of clay, mortar and chalk fragments containing pottery dated to the 14th century.

A fragment of north–south chalk wall recorded in the watching brief area was probably part of the western external wall of Building 5 and suggests an east–west width of 6.0m.

Pottery recovered from contexts associated with Building 5 included Coarse Border ware and Siegburg Unglazed Stoneware, although the presence of what appears to be a Coarse Border ware lobed cup is a curiosity. Lobed cups are usually thin-walled vessels and not a form usually associated with Coarse Border ware, and in all likelihood the sherd is Kingston-type ware that is exceptionally heavily tempered.

Building 6

(Fig 6)

Building 6 was recorded in Trench 3 and also in Pile Hole 8, and also contained evidence for two phases of use. The first phase included the western external wall of the building – a well-built north–south chalk wall whose west face survived to a height of 0.80m and consisted of four courses of ashlar blocks. The east face of the wall was more roughly coursed and had an offset. To the east of this wall were floors of crushed chalk and tile fragments in a possible room area (Room A).

Built over these floors further to the east was a secondary phase of activity which included a north–south chalk wall with some facing along its base and, further to the east, an east–west chalk wall. To the north and south of this wall were hard crushed chalk floors overlaid by peg-tile debris (Rooms B and C). Building 6 probably continued further to the east but all evidence had been removed by a large 20th-century cellar.

Building 6 is probably late 13th or 14th century in date, and cut into the top of the peat deposit seen in Pile Hole 8 and which contained late 13th-century pottery. The building had gone out of use by the late 15th century, when a pit containing pottery and tile was dug through one of its later walls.

Building 7

(Figs 6, 8 and 9)

Building 7 survived as a cellar built of chalk and occasional blocks of greensand and lying to the north of Building 6. Only the western part of Building 7 was examined, which measured c 4.60m across, north–south. Parts of the north, west and south walls were recorded and survived to a height of at least 0.77m (Fig 8). The walls were built of roughly coursed blocks and the southern wall included a gap measuring 0.60m x 0.40m, evidence of an entrance or a window. The cellar was reused at a later date and contained no in situ deposits associated with its primary phase.

To the north of Building 7 a small chute led into either a chalk-lined pit or a drain (Fig 9). The feature was over 0.70m long (the northern end was not seen) by 0.45m wide and 0.60m deep, and was probably a garderobe (or drain) from the building built above the cellar and emptying into the river. This interpretation is supported by the recovery of mineralised seeds of edible fruits from an associated environmental sample. These consisted of hundreds of seeds from elderberries

Fig 8 Building 7 – a partially excavated cellar, looking north-west. The brick floor is a post-medieval reflooring. Scale 0.5m

(*Sambucus nigra* L), and blackberries/raspberries (*Rubus fruticosus/idaeus*) were also present. These fruits would have been available as a wild or cultivated plant resource, both are rich in vitamin C. Many folk remedies recommended making syrups or 'robs' from elderberry juice as cures for coughs and colds (Grieve 1931, 273). They may also have been used in preparing fruit beers, jams and dye. Elderberries dye natural fabrics a dark purple colour and were recommended in Culpeper's herbal as a hair dye (Culpeper 1653, 128).

Also present, in smaller numbers, were mineralised grape (*Vitis vinifera* L) and fig seeds (*Figus carica* L). Dried figs and currants would have been imported dried, at this date, and eaten as pottages or pies during feast and fast days by rich and poor (Wilson 1973, 333). Henbane seeds (*Hyoscyamus niger* L) were present in small numbers. All parts of this plant are poisonous although it had many medicinal and folk uses. In small doses it was reported to have a sedative effect, the roots used as babies' teethers and the seeds when heated and applied to the mouth used to cure toothache (Grieve 1931, 402–3).

The garderobe was an integral part of the Building 7 cellar and the pottery from its backfilling dates the construction of Building 7 to before the 14th century. Building 7 also produced further fragments from a possible Coarse Border ware lobed cup <P3>, a further Coarse Border ware money box <P4> and a near intact Siegburg Stoneware jakobakanne (a tall, slender jug) <P5> (see Fig 10). This small group encapsulates late medieval pottery groups from London. The locally produced wares are largely Surrey Whitewares, with a substantial amount of imported German stoneware present as well.

Building 8
(Fig 6)

Directly to the south of the Building 7 cellar, and possibly related to it, was Building 8. The evidence for Building 8 included an east–west aligned northern external wall constructed of flint and chalk, with a southern return of flint and constructed over a narrow drain or gully. To the east was another southern return wall of flint, although the latter appeared to turn east at its northern end. This wall lay on the alignment of the west wall of Building 6, but was significantly different in construction, suggesting that Building 8 incorporated or extended parts of the building to the south. It was not clear whether the north–south walls of the building were internal or external, but they appeared to define part of a small room or north–south passage 0.90–1.0m wide. No dating was recovered from Building 8, which was sealed by dumps containing late 16th-century pottery.

Building 9
(Fig 6)

The evidence for Building 9 consisted of a well-built, east–west aligned chalk wall *c* 1.10m wide and surviving 0.50m high. The eastern and western extent of the wall was not recorded and

Fig 9 Garderobe and chute on the north side of Building 7, looking south, with backfilled evaluation trench to left. Scale 0.5m

it was not clear whether the building was associated with Building 4 to the east. The size of the wall suggests that it formed an external side of a large building, although truncation meant that this could not be verified. Truncation had also removed any evidence of floors associated with the wall. No associated dating evidence was recovered, although in common with the other chalk-walled buildings from the site a medieval date is likely. Building 9 may have been the brothel known as The Unicorn.

Building 10

(Fig 6)

Building 10 was represented by part of an east–west aligned wall *c* 0.70m wide and consisting of a flint core with chalk facing to either side, the only example of this type of construction seen on the site. To the south of the wall was a floor of crushed chalk. There is the possibility that Building 10 was part of Building 1, elements of which were recorded nearby to the south. The Building 10 floor surface contained four sherds of 12th- and 13th-century pottery.

Open Area 9 phase 1

(Fig 6)

Two phases of Open Area 9 external activity were recorded in Trench 5 to the south of Buildings 5 and 9. Phase 1 was represented by the truncated remains of a vertical-sided cut

with a flat base which contained a waterlain fill. The fill produced a large amount of 14th-century pottery. The feature may have been one of the fish ponds known to exist on Bankside at this time, and was similar to the feature recorded to the south of Building 3 to the north-east.

The Open Area 9 cut feature contained a large group of Surrey Whiteware sherds, some of which were obviously wasters. Surrey White wasters were excavated at 5–15 Bankside in 1981 (Dennis & Hinton 1983, 286), and that range of wasters was similar to the Kingston ware excavated at the kiln site in Eden Street, Kingston upon Thames (Hinton 1980; Miller & Stephenson 1999). The OA9 pottery is similar to the earlier Bankside material. The reason for its presence on Bankside remains unclear. It may have come from a local whiteware kiln on Bankside, but to date there is no archaeological, place-name or documentary evidence for such a kiln. Neutron-activation analysis has shown that there is little discernible difference between the Bankside material and other Surrey Whitewares being made at the time (Cowell in Pearce & Vince 1988), so one alternative hypothesis is that this material was originally from Kingston and was dumped – in the case of 5–15 Bankside, on the foreshore of a creek. It may have come on a boat, perhaps as ballast or part of a cargo of perfect wares, and was subsequently discarded. The similarity with the Eden Street assemblage is quite marked. If the Bankside material was made locally, there must have been some connection between the two sites.

The potter may have migrated from Kingston to be closer to his main market, where the industries were operating at the same time in competition with each other. If this was the case then surely the Kingston pottery would have suffered, on account of the additional distance to bring the products to market. If a Bankside pottery existed, it may have failed to flourish because of the distance and cost of transporting the white-firing Reading Beds clay.

The range of vessels includes bowls (Miller & Stephenson 1999, 24), cooking pots with applied strip (Pearce & Vince 1988, 62), dripping dish, drinking jugs, baluster jugs, cisterns and pipkins (Miller & Stephenson 1999, 26, 18, 19, 26, 21). Cooking pot fragments with thumbed strips, as found at Eden Street, have not been identified, although there were examples with a thumbed cordon under the rim (Miller & Stephenson 1999, 21). The drinking jugs bear a marked similarity to the Eden Street examples; two are substantially complete, <P6> and <P7> (Fig 10), one of which is missing its base, a characteristic sign of differential expansion, as exhibited among the Eden Street assemblages (Miller & Stephenson 1999, 33).

Some sherds display clear signs of being wasters: there is glaze over broken edges where sherds have been used as kiln spacers, or the glaze has seeped into fissures and the pot has subsequently broken at this point of weakness. There are also examples of overfired and discoloured glaze, and a sherd from a jug in which the potter made a hole to lute a handle to the body, and then was subsequently closed, the presence of which is only obvious on the inside <P8> (see Fig 10).

Open Area 9 phase 2

(Fig 6)

A further phase of activity associated with Open Area 9 was dated to the late 15th century and included a large pit containing a very organic fill. The pit was lined with wooden posts and had a possible plank-lined drain entering it from the south-west. An environmental sample from the feature contained the remains of plants of wasteground, scrub and grassland. Some arable weeds were represented, for example corncockle (*Agrostemma githago* L), sheep's sorrel (*Rumex acetosella* L) and fat hen (*Chenopodium album* L). A large number (51–250) of seeds of weld/dyer's rocket (*Reseda luteola* L) were present. These native plants grow in dry grassland often among arable crops (Hanf 1983, 419; Stace 1991, 343). An initial interpretation of the contents of this pit was stable sweepings. The recovery of seeds of disturbed ground and arable weeds could support this as do the large number of fragments of monocot leaves and grass or rush stem fragments, but they are present in too few a number to be sure. Corncockle is a common find among cereal assemblages for this period (Jones 1988, 90) and a well-known crop weed and contaminant of flour. Weld/dyer's rocket seeds, if processed for dye, give a yellow colour (Kenward & Hall 1995, 770) but in this context it

is likely that the seeds came from crop weeds or locally growing plants. Many fig and blackberry/raspberry seeds were present. These could represent cess and show that domestic refuse was also dumped in this pit.

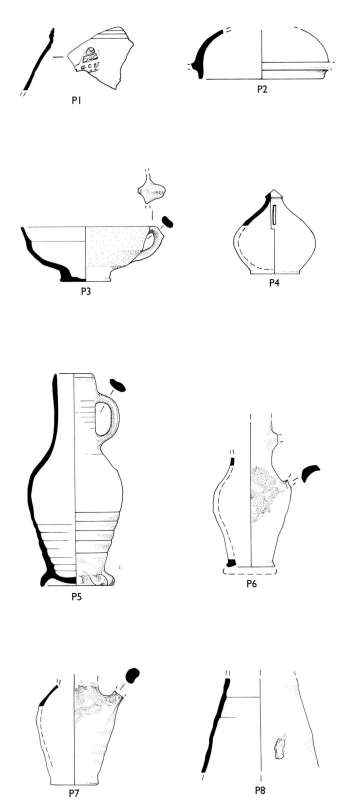

Fig 10 Medieval pottery <P1> – <P8>. Surrey Whitewares: Kingston-type ware jug with stamp <P1>; lid <P2>; ?Coarse Border ware lobed cup <P3>; Coarse Border ware money box <P4>; drinking jugs <P6><P7>; jug sherd showing the closed hole for the handle <P8>. Imported Siegburg Stoneware jakobakanne <P5>. (Scale 1:4)

Nearby was a small pit and a large, linear cut running north-west to south-east which may have been a ditch. The ditch contained seeds mainly from plants of waste and disturbed ground. These included orache (*Atriplex* cf *hastata/patula*), stinging nettle (*Urtica dioica* L), dead-nettle (*Lamium* sp) and curled dock (*Rumex crispus* L). Smaller numbers of elder and fig seeds were present.

Vessels from Open Area 9 phase 2 and worthy of mention include a Kingston ware money box, further evidence of their frequency on Bankside sites. The majority of the pottery was locally produced wares, but with an undercurrent of imports, including Siegburg Stoneware.

Period discussion

(Table 2)

Both the documentary and archaeological evidence point to an extensive phase of development on the site during Period 3, possibly beginning in the early 13th century. Documentary material records activity within the stews in the mid 13th century and this is borne out by the dating evidence presented for the recorded buildings, although Buildings 2 and 10 may have earlier origins.

Although it is difficult to relate buildings known from documents to those recorded on archaeological sites, the fact that the site was in the possession of two property owners may go some way towards identifying some of the buildings recorded. The division between the Crown and the bishop's land (see Fig 5) is based on the information provided by Braines (1924); the transposing of that information on to modern maps is not without difficulties. However, from the information presented it would appear that Buildings 1, 2, 3, 6, 7, 8 and 10 are all located on the bishop's land while Buildings 4, 9 and most of Building 5 are located on Crown land. Unfortunately the configuration of buildings recorded does not tie in with the cartographic evidence (see Figs 11 and 12) but 16th- and 17th-century maps were not accurate. It should also be borne in mind that only fragments of these buildings have been archaeologically recorded and that conjectured wall lines are entirely that.

Documentary evidence indicates that the stewhouse known as The Barge was located to the east of the site but that the stew known as The Bell & Cock was on the site and so, possibly, was the stew known as The Unicorn (see Fig 4). The Unicorn is known to have been on Crown land and (if facing on to the river) is possibly represented by Building 4 or Building 9. It is conceivable that Building 4 is an eastern range to Building 9 and that both of these structures form part of The Unicorn.

The Bell & Cock is known to have been on the bishop's land, presumably fronting Bankside and the Thames, and is possibly represented by Building 2 or Building 3. Evidence from 17th-century documents indicates that The Bell & Cock 'conteyneth in lengthe from outside to outside fiftye and sixe feete of assize, and in bridth from outside to outside sixteene feete of assize' (Collier 1841, 78), but this does not help in deciding between Building 2 or Building 3. However, the fact that Building 2 continues in use into the 16th and 17th centuries may indicate that it is The Bell & Cock.

Table 2 Period 3 dating evidence (13th–15th centuries)

Buildings 3 and 4; Open Area 9				
activity	context	evidence	pot type	date range
Building 3	443	Ceramics	CBW: JUG KING: LID, CUP, ?FINI, JUG, MBOX PMR: -	1270–1400
Building 4	627	Ceramics	CBW: DRIP, FT CP, JUG, JUG STAB FKING: JUG PUZZ KING: BOWL, JUG LOND: RESL	1340–1400
Open Area 9	685	Ceramics	KING: BOWL, CP APST, DISH, DJ, DRIP, JUG, JUG BAL, JUG RND, JUGCIST STAB, MISC, PIP	1300–1400
Open Area 9	682	Ceramics	CBW: JUG KING: ?MBOX LMHG: - LOGR: - SIEG: BEAK PMRE: PIP	1480–1550

The other buildings recorded within this period provide evidence of the development of the site and also suggest that the buildings on Bankside didn't just front on to the river but that there was also 'back yard' development. The recovery of money box fragments from Building 3 (possibly an undocumented stewhouse?) is of interest and may indicate some of the practice within Southwark's brothels. Ceramic money boxes appear to have had only one access – the slot for the money – so the contents could only be retrieved by breaking the vessel. In 16th- and 17th-century playhouses it is thought that the money boxes were used by 'gatherers' to collect entrance fees, with the boxes then 'opened' in the presence of those who had an interest in the contents. It is conceivable that they were used in stewhouses in a similar manner.

2.4 Period 4: 16th and 17th centuries

Documentary evidence

Animal-baiting and the stews

From the Dissolution onwards, the history of landownership on the site becomes increasingly difficult to follow. This is partly due to increasing development on Bankside, resulting in the subdivision of property.

Particular interest in the site in this period is focused on it being the location of a number of animal-baiting arenas. Animal-baiting is an activity that is not properly understood by historians, the study of it suffering from its assumed association with the development of London's early playhouses. This association is due to a number of factors, including the physical proximity of the animal-baiting arenas and playhouses, particularly in the 16th and 17th centuries; the assumed structural parallels between animal-baiting arenas and playhouses; and the connections between personnel involved in animal-baiting and playing in 16th- and 17th-century London.

One connection that appears to apply to both animal-baiting and playing is that both forms of entertainment transcend the supposed barriers between elite and popular culture. Animal-baiting and play-acting were activities used to curry favour at court and with the monarch, yet were in need of noble patronage for their legitimacy. The 1572 Act for the Punishment of Vagabonds stipulated that players and 'bearwards' (see Glossary) who did not 'belong' to a baron or other honourable person were to be deemed vagabonds and would be treated accordingly. In addition to this, both activities were used to entertain visiting foreign dignitaries either at court or at specific purpose-built venues and yet both were practised and developed in front of the paying public.

The exact locations of London's early animal-baiting arenas are not yet fully defined. John Stow, writing in 1598, indicated that the first purpose-built baiting arena was located at the place 'commonly called Paris Garden'. By placing the early baiting arena in Paris Garden, west of Bankside, Stow has caused huge problems for historians as almost all the information indicates that Bankside was the venue for these arenas (see Figs 11 and 12). The combination of a re-examination of the documentary evidence and new archaeological information – presented here for the first time – suggests that Stow's use of language to indicate locations is not always accurate. This re-examination of the evidence sheds new light on the cartographic evidence for early Bankside.

Before looking at the evidence for bearbaiting at Benbow House it is worth considering the available information concerning the stews located on the site.

The early 16th century saw an increase in official interest in the stews, and in 1506 they were closed due to their association with crime and the fear of the spread of disease. The Bell & Cock does not appear to have survived the closure (although the building remained) but The Barge and The Unicorn do, with Carlin indicating that the number of stewhouses was reduced from 18 to 12. After the reopening of the brothels, stewholders were apparently fined for staying open on feast days and other transgressions.

Further evidence of official interest in Bankside is provided by the round-up of suspect persons in the Stews in 1519. This resulted in the arrest of 54 men and women (including one of the king's footmen) (Carlin 1996, 224). The stews were officially suppressed by a proclamation of 13 April 1546 with the Suppression Order stating that 'accustomed assemblies may be in that place thoroughly abolished and extinct' (Carlin 1996, 227).

Five months later, in September 1546, a licence was granted to 'Thomas Fluddie, yeoman of your majesty's bears, to bait and make pastime with your Grace's bears at the accustomed place at London called the Stewes notwithstanding the proclamation'

(Gairdner & Brodie 1910, 88). In the same year 'John Allen, yeoman of my lord prince's bears, [was also licensed] to bait his bears in Southwark or thereabouts, or elsewhere, from time to time, for his most commodity' (Gairdner & Brodie 1910, 328). Despite the reference to the Stews being the accustomed place for bearbaiting there seems to be no documentary evidence to support this, and the earliest documentary evidence for animal-baiting in Southwark appears to be the 1542 manuscript map of Southwark. This map locates a bullring along the west side of Borough High Street with the location supported by an indenture, dated 17 April 1561. The indenture states that Christopher Rolle sold to George Thompson, of St George's Southwark, carpenter, and Johane, his wife, 'all those fourteene tenementes, or cotages and gardeyns, commonly called the Bulryng, sett, lying and beyng on the strete syde, by the alley called the Bullryng, in the Parishe of St George, in Southwark' (Rendle 1878, 31). Wyngaerde's panorama of 1544–8, showing the southern approaches to London Bridge, does show a structure that can be identified as a bullring.

Bearbaiting on Bankside

At the Dissolution many properties in Southwark were leased or sold to the former tenants (Carlin 1996, 63) and in 1540 Bishop Stephen Gardiner transferred The Bell & Cock and The Barge to William Payne. The description of the lease locates the land as bounded by Bankside to the north, the tenement called The Rose to the east, the property of the nuns of Stratford Priory (ie the Polsted lease) to the west and Maiden Lane (ie Park Street) to the south. Braines suggests that the northern, western and eastern boundary descriptions are correct but that the location of the southern boundary along Maid Lane is incorrect and that the southern boundary was much further north, that is, at the southern boundary of the bishop of Winchester's land (see Fig 5).

The prioress of Stratford's land (which became Crown land and surrounded the bishop's holdings) was granted, at the Dissolution, to Ralph Sadler (Braines 1924, 91). Sadler sold it to Henry Polsted on 29 February 1538/9. By this acquisition, Polsted, who had previously purchased The Rose from William Spence (see above), now owned land which enclosed the bishop of Winchester's land on the east, south and west, and thus owned the western part of the Benbow House site.

In Polsted's lease from the Crown in 1552, the property is described (Braines 1924, 92) as comprising:

i) a capital curtilage called 'le Beare yarde' with 'le Berehouse' and garden in the possession of John Allen
ii) 4 messuages with gardens and wharves in the possession of Robert Mole
iii) a messuage, curtilage and garden in the possession of Robert Johnson
iv) a garden called 'le Rose garden' in the possession of Leonard Willis

v) a messuage called 'le Rose' in the possession of John Dauncie

vi) the ferm of a capital messuage or inn called 'le Unicorn' with garden adjoining

vii) a messuage called 'Fluddies' in the possession of Thomas Warren

viii) two messuages lying together, with garden in the possession of Thomas Fluddye

ix) a messuage and garden in the possession of Robert Exninge

x) a garden called 'le Kinges Pike garden' in the possession of Peter Hunnye and

xi) a messuage next adjoining in the possession of Peter Hunnye

The first item of interest is the description of John Allen's holding as being a 'beare yarde' and 'berehouse'. This latter spelling has occasionally led to confusion but the fact that the property was in the possession of John Allen, who had been licensed to bait bears in Southwark or thereabouts in 1546, may indicate the presence of a bear house and yard on the Polsted property. The *Survey of London* (1950, 67) points out that by 1620 the term 'bear gardens' appears to have become a generic term for the sheds and kennels, as well as the rings and adjoining houses. Whether this applied more than 70 years earlier is difficult to say.

Items (vii) and (viii) are also of interest. Item (vii) refers to a messuage called Fluddies now in the possession of Thomas Warren, while item (viii) indicates that Thomas Fluddye is in

possession of two messuages with a garden. It would appear likely that this is the same Thomas Fluddie, Yeoman of His Majesty's Bears, who had been licensed to bait and 'make pastime' with bears at the accustomed place at London called the Stewes. Not only is the Master of the King's Bears in possession of a tenancy of part of the Polsted property, but the Yeoman of the Prince's Bears (John Allen) is in possession of a 'beare yarde' and 'berehouse'.

The identification of a bearbaiting arena on the Polsted lease may go some way to clearing up the confusion over the location of Southwark's bear gardens. Carlin (1996, 213 n 23), in discussing the land leased from the bishops by William Payne, states that Payne built the 'Bankside bear garden partly on this site and partly on an adjoining site, which had been owned by the prioress and nuns of Stratford-at-Bow [*ie* the Polsted lease] and had contained fish ponds and the Unicorn stewhouse'. How William Payne managed to build a baiting arena on his land and on land belonging to Polsted does not seem to have been addressed and it would seem possible that two baiting arenas existed – one on the Polsted land and one on the land leased by William Payne. It is possible that these are the two arenas illustrated on the map attributed to Ralph Agas (Fig 11).

In a similar vein, the *Survey of London* (1950, 67) relating the evidence in a dispute between the Crown and bishop of Winchester, over ownership of land 'in the neighbourhood of the Bear Gardens', states that witnesses in the dispute appear to agree that the bear gardens were either on the bishop's land, leased to William Payne in 1540 and formerly known as The Barge, Bell & Cock, or on the king's land leased in 1552

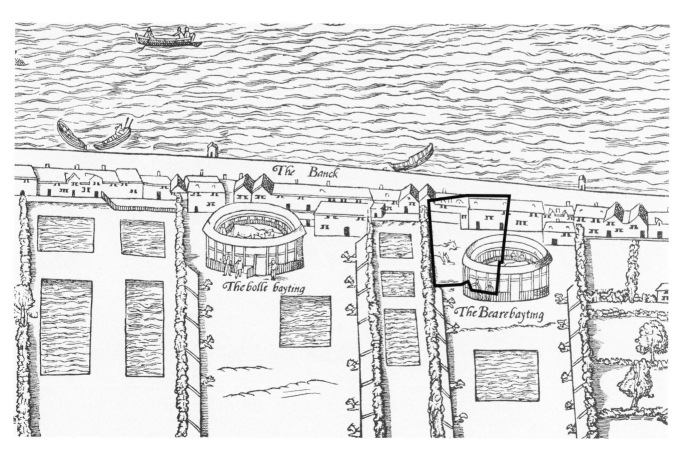

Fig 11 Civitas Londini map of Bankside 1560–90 attributed to Ralph Agas

to Henry Polsted and formerly known as The Unicorn and The Rose. The witnesses in the dispute were, presumably, relying on fading memories and may have been confused over the location of the animal-baiting arenas. That Payne had an interest in bearbaiting is not at issue as in 1560 (and possibly earlier) he was deputy to Cuthbert Vaughan, Master of the Bears.

The role of the Master of the Bears is discussed in detail by Susan Cerasano (1991) although it is worth summarising some of the detail here. The office of Master of the Bears is traceable to 1484 and by the time of Henry VIII 'was well established within the Court hierarchy' (Cerasano 1991, 195). When Elizabeth I granted the Mastership to Ralph Bowes (in 1573) he was described as 'Chief Master Overseer and Ruler of all and singular our game'. Remuneration appears to have been small but the appointment was a royal one and the Master had the sole right to license bearwards and was expected to make his own profits by whatever means he chose. While the Master was allowed to hire his own deputy, the positions of Sergeant of Bears and Yeoman of Bears were Crown appointments.

In addition to licensing bearwards the Master of the Bears was also able to commission the collection of dogs to undertake the baiting. Dogs were apparently collected throughout the country – the papers of Edward Alleyn and Philip Henslowe, who obtained joint Mastership of the Bears in November 1604, include discussion about the collection of dogs from as far afield as Kent and Lancashire. In the draft of a letter (dated June 1607) from Alleyn and Henslowe to their deputy Christopher Goffe, they commission him to find dogs that will perform any service his majesty commands and direct him to dispatch dogs to their office 'att pallas garden between Easter and whisuntid' (Greg 1975, 104). Greg includes the information that on the back of the first leaf of the letter are some accounts for bear's meat at 'Dartford, Gravesend, Rochester, Maydstone, Sittingborne, ffeversham, Caunterbury, Dover, ffolstone, Ashford, Wye', which may imply that Henslowe and Alleyn were dealing in bear's meat to raise further revenue. The issue of where the dogs were to be directed to is dealt with below.

The information that William Payne built a bear garden on Bankside came from the evidence given by John Taylor in 1620, as part of the dispute between the Crown and the bishop of Winchester over ownership of land 'in the neighbourhood of the Bear Gardens'. Witnesses called in the dispute were asked a series of questions set by each side and their responses were recorded. Taylor, who was 77 years old at the time, answered some of the questions from the Crown and provided the information that Payne had died 'about forty years since' and that he had lived in a house called The Dancing Bears. The *Survey of London* (1950, 68) records that William Payne died in 1575 and that either he or his son John built a bear garden on the bishop's land. Taylor continued that Payne built a 'place to bait the bears' close to that house 'in the outer court towards the Thames northwards from the now Hope playhouse', that it was on the bishop's land and that he had seen the lease and heard it read (Kingsford 1920, 176). In response to questions about the name and builder(s) of the bear garden, Payne responded that it was known as

'Mr Payne's standings' and that either William Payne or Simon Poulton erected them. Chambers (1923, vol 2, 451 n 2) records that William Payne and one Simon Powlter were licensed to bait bears up to c 1574 and that Powlter was receiving payment as Yeoman of Bears in 1571 (450 n 4). In response to questions on behalf of the bishop of Winchester, Taylor stated that he had seen the lease, dated 1540, from Bishop Gardiner to William Payne and that bears had been baited in four separate places on Bankside – at Mason's stairs, near Maid Lane by the corner of the Pike Garden, on William Payne's lease and at the site of the Hope. Chambers (1923, vol 2, 462) includes the information that the depositions include mention of a bull house built in a dog yard, a hay house, a pond to wash the bears in and a pond for dead dogs! The Agas map shows a pond south of the bearbaiting arena.

Although the deposition of a 77-year-old man may be called into question, the evidence presented by Taylor is useful in interpreting other documentary sources. His evidence is consistent with our information. The baiting place 'near Maid Lane by the corner of the Pike Garden' is located on land that formerly belonged to the prioress of Stratford and was subsequently leased to Henry Polsted. This is presumably where John Allen and Thomas Fluddie were involved in the baiting of bears and is consistent with the locations mentioned in their licences. Payne's standings, on Payne's lease from the bishop of Winchester, were erected not later than 1573 (Kingsford 1920, 169), the year in which Polsted's 21-year lease of his land expired and the year in which Ralph Bowes received the grant of Master of the Bears from Elizabeth I. The combination of the expiring of Polsted's lease and the appointment of a new Master of Bears may suggest that Kingsford is correct in his suggested date for Payne's construction. Where Payne built his arena is not certain although timber piles sealed by clay (see Building 12 below) appear to provide crucial evidence. As will be seen below, Payne's standings collapsed in 1583.

Unfortunately there appears to be no evidence about the fate of Polsted's lease between 1573 and 11 October 1595, when Elizabeth I granted the land to Robert Liveseye and Gerrard Gore, while retaining one tenement and a parcel of land and ponds called the Queen's Pike Garden (Braines 1924, 92).

In the late 16th or early 17th century Philip Henslowe acquired the lease of land which had previously been leased from the Crown by Liveseye and Gore. Braines (1924, 92) suggests that Henslowe acquired the lease in 1605, whereas the *Survey of London* (1950, 69) states that Henslowe acquired the lease in 1596. Henslowe's lease of the Liveseye and Gore land passed, at his death, to his widow Agnes, then to her daughter Joan (wife of Edward Alleyn) and so to Alleyn (Braines 1924, 94). Whether Polsted (and subsequently Liveseye and Gore) acquired all of the prioress of Stratford's land is not certain, as Chambers (1924, vol 2, 464) records that at the Dissolution a tenement, to the west of The Barge and Bell & Cock, once held by the prioress, passed to the Crown and then to Thomas and Isabella Keyes. The Keyes' holding (The Unicorn?) had apparently come into Henslowe's hand by 1597 but prior to that both Morgan Pope and Thomas Burnaby had some of the Keyes' land on sublease and Burnaby probably had all of the Keyes' lease itself.

That there were two bear gardens within the vicinity of the site also appears to be supported by other land transactions. In August 1578 one Thomas Stone let, to Richard Ballard, land described as a garden plot, 'sometimes parcel of the old Beare Garden' (Kingsford 1920, 172). Nine years later, in October 1587, John Bixon assigned Ballard's lease to Morgan Pope and used the same description, and this lease eventually came into the hands of Edward Alleyn. Alleyn endorsed the Bixon assignment as 'The lease of my garden by the beare-garden' (Alleyn was at the time in possession of Payne's lease with its bear gardens), suggesting that it relates to a baiting arena other than Payne's standings.

Further evidence of two bearbaiting pits is provided by John Stow who, in discussing Bankside, states that 'there be two Beare gardens, the olde and the new places, whering be kept Beares, Buls and other beastes to be bayted. As also Mastiues in severall kenels, nourished to baite them. These Beares and other Beasts are there bayted in plottes of ground, scaffolded about for the Beholders to stand safe. Next on this banke was sometime the Bordello or stewes' (Kingsford 1908, vol 2, 54).

Bearbaiting: spectators and structure

Graphic evidence of the dangers of baiting is relayed by Kingsford (1920, 162). In an incident that occurred on Bankside on 9 December 1554, a blind bear broke loose and bit a man who later died of his wounds. The dangers of attending large public gatherings in purpose-built timber structures are shown by the events of Sunday 13 January 1583, when the bear gardens collapsed killing seven people outright. It is worth looking at part of John Field's account of the 1583 collapse. Field was a preacher and 'castigator of the stage' who railed against abuses of the Sabbath and considered the collapse to be part of God's judgement. John Field's 'exhortation' provides valuable information about the type of structure used for bearbaiting, the audience and evidence of events on William Payne's lease. Field estimated that about a thousand people were present when the structure collapsed. He writes:

Beeing thus ungodly assembled, to so unholy a spectacle ... the yeard, standings, and galleries being ful fraught ... This gallery that was double, and compassed the yeard round about, was so shaken at the foundation, that it fell (as it were in a moment) flat to the ground, without post or peere, that was left standing, so high as the stake whereunto the Beare was tied ... In the fal of it, there were slaine five men and two women ... to wit, Adam Spencer a Felmonger, in Southwarke, William Cockram a Baker, dwelling in Shordich, John Burton Cleark, of S Marie Wolmers in Lombard strete, Mathew Mason, servant with Master Garland, dwelling in Southwarke, Thomas Peace, servant with Rober Tasker, dwelling in Clerken well. The maydens names, Alice White, servant to a Pursemaker without Cripplegate, and Marie Harrison, daughter to John Harrison, being a waterbearer, dwelling in Lombard streat ... Of all the multitude there, which must needed be farre above a

thousande, it is thought by the judgement of most people, that not the third personne escaped unhurt. But it shoulde appere that they were most hurt and in danger, which stood under the Galleries on the ground, upon whom both the waight of Timbre and people fel ... For surely it is to be feared, beesides the distruction bothe of bodye and soule, that many are brought unto, by frequenting the Theater, the Curtin and such like. (Chambers 1923, vol 4, 219–21)

Field's description of the structure, the occupations of the people killed and the fact that most injuries occurred to people who stood under the galleries may provide some information about social divisions among the audience at bearbaitings. From available information, particularly the diary of Alessandro Magno on his visit to London in 1562, baiting arenas had a similar pricing policy to that later used in playhouses. Magno records that 'to enter below one pays a penny ... and two to go up into the stands' (Dawson 1964, 99). It is possible that the wealthier members of the audience would pay the extra penny for exclusivity and safety. Indeed it has been argued that until the middle of the 16th century bullbaiting was a commercial necessity and bearbaiting was a sport of the privileged (Brownstein 1969, 244), and the rationale for bullbaiting appears to be connected more to the preparation and sale of the meat than with public entertainment. Evidence records penalties levied for the sale of unbaited bull's meat, and Pearce (1929, 76) in his history of the Butchers' Company, records that in 1582/3 'Hy. Baker [was fined] for kellynge a bull unbeayted – 2/' [two shillings].

That the 1583 collapse took place at 'Payne's standings' and that it led to an immediate rebuilding of a baiting arena 'larger in Circuit and compasse', with galleries instead of the standings, similar to the three-storeyed amphitheatre playhouses in the northern suburbs (Brownstein 1969, 249), does not appear to be in doubt. It is presumably the new structure that is illustrated by John Norden in his *Speculum Britanniae* map of 1593 (Fig 12).

Paris Garden and Bankside

The arguments concerning the misidentification of the baiting pits on Bankside with the manor of Paris Garden are dealt with by Kingsford (1920), Chambers (1923, vol 2, 458–62) and Brownstein (1969). In addition to their arguments, the cartographic evidence for Paris Garden provides no evidence of animal-baiting structures.

One likely explanation for the references to Paris Garden appears to be the usage of terms to describe locations and the means of access to Bankside. Chambers suggests that the practice of baiting bears by the Thames, which appears to be a phenomenon associated with the monarch and visiting dignitaries, was associated with Paris Garden as that was where the king's barge was moored. Spectators to baiting by the Thames were carried on barges that were presumably boarded at the moorings at Paris Garden, hence people reporting that they watched baiting at Paris Garden. It would still appear,

Fig 12 Speculum Britanniae map of Bankside 1593 by John Norden

however, that the baiting actually took place within the vicinity of Bankside as an account of Henry VIII watching a baiting in July 1539, in his barge with a great number of barges and boats about him, records the baiting 'over against the Bank' (Chambers 1923, vol 2, 460). Interestingly the maps of Agas and Braun and Hogenberg show Paris Garden as having a larger landing stage/jetty than anywhere on Bankside.

Even Philip Henslowe and Edward Alleyn appear to have had some difficulty with understanding the difference between Bankside and Paris Garden. In the draft of their letter to Christopher Goffe, dated June 1607 (see above), they command him to arrange for the dispatch of dogs to 'our office att pallas garden' (Greg 1975, 104). However, letters that are addressed to and received by Henslowe and Alleyn are directed in 1593 to 'E Alline on bankside' (Greg 1975, 34), and to 'mr hinslo ... dwelling on the bank sid right over against the clink' in the same year (Greg 1975, 36). But in April 1609 Patrick Brewe, who leased tenements near the Fortune playhouse from Alleyn, addressed a letter to Edward Alleyn 'nere unto pallace garden' (Greg 1975, 15). In 1609 there is no doubt that all the baiting arenas are on Bankside, no matter where Alleyn lived at that time.

Philip Henslowe and Edward Alleyn

William Payne died in 1574/5 and his widow leased The Barge to Francis Puckryche. Payne was succeeded (as Deputy Master of Bears) by a man called Wistoe (also Wistow and Wiston), and it was either Wistoe or Morgan Pope who erected the new bear garden, on the bishop's land, after the 1583 collapse. Chambers (1923, vol 2, 451 n 2) notes that between *c* 1585 and 1587 John Napton and Morgan Pope were the people licensed to bait bears on Bankside. Joan Payne's lease to Francis Puckryche, dated 11 November 1574, locates The Barge with The Rose to its east, a tenement (The Bell & Cock?) in the occupation of John Brewes to the west, the wharf to the north and the bear house, in the occupation of William Glover and Joan Gravesend, to the south. Puckryche's lease was to be active from Christmas Day 1574 and last for 21 years.

However, on 1 August 1582 Joan Payne assigned the leases of The Barge and The Bell & Cock to John White and John Malthouse with White's half subsequently being assigned to Malthouse on 5 February 1589 (Greg 1908, 25). On 28 November 1595 Philip Henslowe bought the lease from Malthouse for six pounds. In the record of the agreement it is described as 'consaring a bargen of the beargarden' (Foakes & Rickert 1961, 74) but presumably refers to properties at the north of the bear garden, fronting on to Bankside. That this is the case appears to be borne out by Henslowe's record of income from rent for the year 1602 which includes, under the heading 'Mr Malthouses rents' (*ie* The Barge and The Bell & Cock):

wm glover	liijs iiijd [53s 4d]
E Alleyn	x*li* [£10]
Simon Birde	xxvjs 8d [26s 8d]
wm Tyghton	xxvjs 8d [26s 8d]

(*li* = *librae* (pounds); Foakes & Rickert 1961, 247)

Glover's rent in 1602, although twice that of Birde and Tyghton, appears to be for a tenement within The Barge or Bell & Cock and not for the bear garden itself.

The presence of Edward Alleyn in a 'former' Bankside stew is of interest in the light of a letter from Edward Alleyn to his wife (Philip Henslowe's stepdaughter) Joan Woodward. In the letter, dated 2 May 1593 (Foakes & Rickert 1961, 274), Alleyn refers to the fact that his wife has been 'carted' (carried in a cart through the streets as a punishment) and promises to gain revenge against those who carted her. Collier (1841, 24) suggests that Joan Woodward was carted for 'infringement of the order against dramatic performances', although carting was often used as a punishment for offences related to prostitution. Burford (1993, fig 8) refers to her as a whoremistress. It is also of interest to note the amount of rent that Alleyn was paying (£10 as opposed to Glover's £2 13s 4d and Birde's and Tyghton's £1 6s 8d). The comparison of Alleyn's high rent with the documented case of Thomas Dyconson who, in 1481, leased a brothel from the churchwardens of St Margaret's at a higher than normal rent (Carlin 1996, 214 n 28) is of interest.

In 1586 Morgan Pope was paying tithes for the bear garden having 'obtained an exemplification of the grant of mastership of the Game of Bears' in 1585 (*Survey of London* 1950, 68) and from 1590 Thomas Burnaby, licensed to bait bears between 1590 and 1594, began to acquire and lease property around the bear gardens. Burnaby bought the lease of the bear garden on the bishop's property in 1590 and immediately let it to Richard Reve, for a yearly rent of £120, under the description of 'all that Tenemente whearein one John Napton deceased did latelie inhabyte ... on the Bankesyde ... Togeather wth the Beare garden and the Scaffoldes houses game and dogges and all other thinges thereunto apperteyninge ... excepting such fees as shal be ... payable to the maister of the said game.' The schedule of stock included in the lease consisted of:

one Brinded Bull, the pryce , v. *li* [£5]
one blacke Bull called Danyell, at iiij. *li* [£4]
one great beare called Tom Hunckes, x. *li* [£10]
one greate beare called Harry of Tame, at viij. *li* [£8]
one red Bull called Jugler, at iiij. *li* [£4]
one greate beare called Harry of Warwicke, viij. *li* [£8]
one greate beare called Jeremy, at viij. *li* [£8]
one greate beare called Sampson, at viij. *li* [£8]
one beare called Danyell, at vj. *li* [£6]
one she beare called Bosse, at v. *li* [£5]
one yonge he beare called Whitinge, iij. *li* [£3]
one old she beare called Nan, xxx. s [30s]
one horse and the ape, at xl. s [40s]
one Pudding boate, [?] ij. *li* [£2]

[Kingsford (1920, 174) includes a note to say that the manuscript is defective.]

Edward Alleyn purchased Burnaby's interest in the bear garden for £200 in 1594 and operated there under a licence from the Master, Ralph Bowes. With Henslowe's acquisitions in 1595 they began to pursue their interest in the Mastership of the Bears which they eventually obtained on 28 November 1604 from Sir William Steward (or Stuart) whom Chambers (1923, vol 2, 452) refers to as 'an invading Scot'. Once they had the Mastership of the Bears and a tight grip on the property surrounding the bear garden, Henslowe's and Alleyn's income was derived from at least seven sources at the bear garden, namely (Cerasano 1991, 203):

the leases to property that surrounded the bear garden
the licences granted to individuals to bait at the bear garden
the matches that they ran themselves at the bear garden
the profits made on betting for all matches at the bear garden
fees collected for entertainment at court and at the Tower
licences granted to itinerant bearwards
fees collected from the export and sale of mastiffs

The activities of Joan Woodward may have added an extra source to their income.

Henslowe records the following income from the bear garden, in 1608, 'beginning at Chrystmas holedayes as foloweth':

Rd one Monday St steuenes daye   iiij *li* [£4]
Rd one tewesdaye St Johnes daye   vj *li* [£6]
Rd one wensday beinge Chilldermas daye   iij *li* xiij s [£3 13s]

Henslowe also records his income from the Fortune playhouse (north of the Thames) on the same days as follows (Foakes & Ricket 1961, 264):

Rd one St steuenes daye   xxv s [25s]
Rd one St Johnes daye   xxxxv s [45s]
Rd one Chelldermas daye   xxxxiiij s ix d [44s 9d]

It would appear that, in 1608 at least, the bear garden was more lucrative than the Fortune.

Two years after gaining the Mastership of the Bears, Henslowe and Alleyn contracted Peter Street to redevelop the properties that fronted on to Bankside. The contract is worth examining for the information it may throw on archaeological remains recorded towards the northern end of the Benbow House site. It is reproduced from Collier (1841, 78–81):

This indenture made the second day of June 1606 ...
Betwene Peter Streete, cittizen and carpenter of London
on thone party, and Phillip Henslowe and Edward Alleyn,
of the parish of St Saviors in Southwark in the County of
Surrey ... Witnessethe that ... the said Peter Streete, before
the thirde day of September next comynge, shall at his
owne proper costes and charges, not only take and pull
downe for ... Phillip Henslowe and Edward Alleyn, so
much of the tymber or carpeneters work of the foreside of
the messuage or tenemente called the Beare garden, next

the river of Thames in the parishe of St Saviors aforesaide, as conteyneth in lengthe from outside to outside fiftye and sixe feete of assize [measurement], and in bridth from outside to outside sixteene feete of assize; but also in steade and place thereof, before the saide thirde day of September, att his or their like costes and charges, shall well sufficiently, and workmanlike, make or erect sett up and fully finishe one new frame for a house, to conteyne in lengthe from outside to outside fiftie and sixe feete of assize, and in bridth from outside to outside sixteene foote of assize, which frame shalbe made of good, new sufficient and sounde Tymber of oke, to be fynished in all thinges as hereunder mentioned; that is to say: that the saide frame shall conteyne in height two storyes and a halfe, the whole two storyes of the same frame to be in height from flower to flower ten foote of assize a peece, and the halfe storey to be in height fower foote of assize, and all the principall rafters of the same frame to be framed with crooked posts and bolted with ironbolts through the rafters, which ironbolts are to be provided at the cotses and charges of the saide Peter Streete his executors or assignes. And also shall make in the same frame throughout the two flowers with good and sufficient joystes, the same flowers to be boarded throughout with good and sounde deal bordes to be plained and closely laid and shott. All the principall longe upright postes of the said frame to be nyne ynches broade and seaven ynches thicke: and shall make in the same frame three maine summers [bearing beams], that is to say in the uppermost story twoe summers and in the lower story one summer, every summer to be one foote square; all the brest summers to be eight ynches broade and seaven ynches thick. The same frame to jetty over towardes the Thames one foote of assize. And also shall make on the south side of the saide frame a sufficient staire case, with staires convenient to leade up into the uppermost romes of the saide frame, with convenient dores out of the same staire case into every of the rooms adjoining thereunto, and in every rome of the saide frame one sufficient dore; and also by the same staire case shall make and frame one studdy, with a little rome over the same, which studdy is to jetty out from the same frame fower foote of assize, and to extend in lengthe from the said staire case unto the place where the chimneyes are appoynted to be sett, with a sufficient door into either of the romes of the same studdy. And the nether [lower] story of the same frame shall seperate and devide into fower romes: that is to say, the first towards the east to be for a tenemente, and to conteyne in length from wall to wall thirteene foote of assize; the next rome to be for a gate rome, and to coteyne in length ten foote of assize; the third rome twenty foote of assize and the fowerth westward, thirteene foote of assize. And the second story shall seperate into three romes, the first over the rome appoynted for a tenemente on the east end of the said frame, to conteyne in length thirteene foote of assize, the midle rome thirty foote of assize, and the third rome westward thirtene foot likewise of assize. And

the halfe story above to be divided into two romes, namely over the said tenement thirteene foote, to be seperated from the rest of the said frame, and the residue to be open in one rome only. And out of the said frame towardes the Thames shall make twoe dores, and one faire paire of gates with two wickettes proportionable. And also att either end of the lower storey of the same frame shall make one clere story window [to] either of the same clere storyes, to be in height three foote of assize, and sixe foote in length, and in the middle rome of the same frame, conteyning twenty foote, to have a clere story windowe throughout the height of the said former clere storyes: and in the second story of the same frame shall make three splay windowes, every windowe to be sixe foote betweene the posts; and in the same second story shall make seaven clere story windowes, every clere story to be three foote wide a peece, with one mullion in the midest of every clere story; and every of the same clere storyes to be three foote and a halfe in depth. And over the foresaid gate shall make one greete square windowe, to be in length ten foote of assize and to jetty over from the said frame three foote of assize, standing upon twoe carved Satyres, the same window to be in wheight accordinge to the depth of the story, and the same window to be framed with twoe endes with mullions convenient; and over the same windowe to be framed one piramen with three piramides, the same frame to have fower gable endes towards the Thames, and upon the top of every gable end one piramide and between every gable end to be left three foote for the falling of the water and in every gable end one clere story, and backward over the gable of the same frame towardes the south one gable end with a clere story therein, and under the same gable and backward in the second story one clere storey windowe. And also in that parcell of the saide frame as is appoynted for a tenement shall make twoe pairs of staires, one over another by the place where the chimneyes are appoynted to be sett. And that he the saide Peter Streete, his executors administrators or assigns, shall before the saide thirde day of September next comynge after the date hereof fully furnishe the saide frame in and by all thinges as aforesaid, and all other carpenters worke specified in a plott made of the said frame, subscribed by the saide Peter and by him delivered to the said Phillip Henslowe and Edward Alleyn, in such comely and convenient manner and sorte as by the same plott is figured, without fraud or covyn, and at his of their owne charges shall fynd all nayles to be used in and about the carpenters worke of the same frame.

Whether Peter Street remained within the budget that Henslowe and Alleyn had set him is not known, but in his accounts, Alleyn records the fact that he spent £360 for the building of houses, presumably connected with the bear garden, in 1607/8. In fact, the way in which he entered his accounts appears to imply that he didn't spend any money in 1606, despite Street being contracted to finish the new building in September of that year.

By 1613 the bear garden was presumably suffering from almost 30 years of use and on 29 August of that year, Henslowe entered into a contract with Jacob Meade and Gilbert Katherens (carpenter) to pull down the bear gardens and erect a playhouse modelled on the Swan. The new playhouse was to have a movable stage so that the building could be used for baiting. It is this 1613 construction that we know as the Hope. Although the Hope was finally built off the bishop of Winchester's land, there are a number of factors in the Hope contract that are of interest to the bear garden. Katherens was contracted to pull down the bear garden 'wherin Beares and Bulls have been heretofore usuallie bayted' and to pull down a stable 'wherin Bulls and horsses did usuallie stande'. He was also instructed to use all the 'tymber benches seates, slates, tyles Brickes and all other thinges belonginge to the saide Game place or Bull house or stable, And also all suche olde tymber whiche the saide Phillipe Henslowe hathe latelie bought beinge of an old house in Thames street, London, whereof moste parte is now lyinge in the Yarde or Backsyde of the saide Bearegarden' (Greg 1907, 19–22). Obviously some of the raw material of the bear garden was reusable.

Philip Henslowe died in January 1616, with an estate valued at £1700 12s 8d. Greg (1908, 26) says that The Barge, The Bell & Cock and The Unicorn (the Keyes lease!) were sold by Henslowe's executors 'to meet the legacies bequeathed in his will' and ultimately came into the possession of Edward Alleyn (Cerasano 1994, 30–1 n 13).

After the death of Henslowe and Alleyn the 'unification' of the Polsted and Payne leases begins to fracture along the original lease lines.

Pothouses and glasshouses

On 13 June 1635/6 the Liveseye/Gore lease (see above) of the Polsted property was granted by King Charles I, on perpetual lease, to Richard Sydenham and Edward Smith, whose interest was acquired by John Squibb. Some 35 years later Charles II disposed of the land and on 17 January 1671/2 the trustees sold, to Robert, son of John Squibb, the freehold of the property described as 'all those messuages, cottages, curtilages, wharfes, barnes, orchards, gardens and other heriditaments whatsoever ... now or late in the tenure ... of John Allan, Robert Mole: and all the other tenants mentioned in the Polsted lease' (Braines 1924, 94).

On 1 August 1671, John Squibb leased part of his property to William Lillington (Lillingston, according to Braines) and others. Braines (1924, 98) says that at the time Squibb leased the land to Lillingston, a pothouse and glasshouse were already standing, although the exact date of their construction is not known.

The Chancery Proceedings of 1705 cite the 1671 lease detailing a pothouse, outhouse and appurtenances formerly in the tenure of Francis Mercer, potter (Britton 1987, 47). From the evidence presented by Frank Britton, it would appear that by 1695 Moses Johnson was the potter, as he had been

financed by Richard White of the Montague Close pottery, to 'start a stoneware pottery in the Bear Garden' (1987, 47). In that year (ie 1695) John Dwight (of Fulham?) brought actions against Johnson and White 'for infringing his stoneware patent'. Whether Dwight's action caused Johnson to alter his production methods is not yet known but in 1702 Ferdinando Parkhurst was running the pottery, described as a 'Holland Potter'. This would imply that Parkhurst was making tin-glazed earthenware (also known as delftware) pottery. In 1710, the pottery was advertised to be let. The advertisement referred to the premises as 'several Warehouses and other large Buildings Yards and Conveniences, formerly a Pot-house, lately a Glass House ... near the Bankside at the Bear Garden Stairs' (Britton 1987, 47). It would appear that prior to 1710, the pottery had gone out of business to be replaced by glass manufacturers.

Likewise, the origins of the glasshouse are uncertain and it may be that John Bowles, recorded as being in partnership with William Lillington at the Stony Street Glasshouse in 1678 (Buckley 1930, 138), may already have been in tenure when Lillington took part of the lease from Squibb. Certainly by 1684, Bowles is recorded as being 'Master of several Glasshouses at St Mary Overye's and the Bear Gardens in Southwark, for the making of Green glass', that is, bottles (Buckley 1930, 145 n 19).

The Bear Gardens glasshouse was apparently extended, by John Bowles, at the end of the 17th century (Survey of London 1950, 70). Frank Britton (1987, 47), using the records of the Clink Court Leet, notes that between 1707 and 1709 the court recorded the regular fining, for excessive smoke, of two glasshouses in Bear Gardens. Watts (1990, 208) states that two Bear Gardens glasshouses, built by Bowles, were 'repeatedly fined for nuisance caused by smoke at both premises'.

The output of the glasshouses appears to have varied over the years, with Bowles 'establishing' glass bottlemaking there before 1684 and subsequently experimenting in making window glass which he called 'Crown Glass' (Buckley 1930, 139). Bowles appears to have continued manufacturing window glass at the Bear Gardens until 1691 when he moved his production to Ratcliff, north of the Thames, and assigned his interest in the Bear Gardens glasshouse to a syndicate that included Robert Hookes and Christopher Dodsworth.

On 12 June 1691 Hookes and Dodsworth obtained a 14-year patent for the manufacture of 'fine window glass and "casting glass and particularly looking glass plates"', (Buckley 1930, 139) but apparently waited another 12 months before taking orders on their patented products.

In 1717 the Bear Gardens glasshouse was up for lease again with enquiries about the lease to be addressed to Mr Clyatt in New Thames Street, and on 1 June 1720 the 'Company' at the Bear Gardens glasshouse posted a notice in the Daily Courant to say that they 'have made, and do continue to make the finest of Crown Glass' (Buckley 1930, 146 n 29).

The end date of the Bear Gardens glasshouses is uncertain. That they certainly did not exist by 1776 and possibly did not exist by 1748 will be shown below.

Archaeological evidence

Building 2 phase 2

(Fig 13)

Although the first phase of Building 2 had apparently been at least partly demolished in the late 15th century, a later phase of Building 2 was recorded and consisted of two parallel, east–west aligned chalk and flint walls. The northernmost of the two overlay the south wall of Building 2 phase 1, while the southernmost was 1.20m to the south (Fig 13). The walls are difficult to interpret as so little was seen of them but they appear to have been related to a structure added to the south side of Building 2 phase 1. The primary phase of Building 2 may have been one of the buildings documented as being demolished at Bear Gardens in 1606, but the original foundations could have been reused for the new building erected by Peter Street in this area and which is known to have had a staircase on its south side. It is possible that the phase 2 walls were associated with the external staircase for this new property. Unfortunately no dating was recovered from associated contexts.

Building 11

(Fig 13)

Building 11 postdated the disuse of Building 4 and overlay the south-western part of the earlier building plot. A north–south aligned east wall and east–west aligned north wall met to form the north-east corner of the building. The walls were constructed of chalk, flint and ragstone fragments. It is possible that Building 11 was built against the retained north wall of Building 5. The function of Building 11 is unknown, although its small size and relatively poor build suggest that it may have been domestic. Alternatively it may have been one of the many dog kennels that were associated with the animal-baiting arenas on Bankside. Postholes located just to the east may have been related to the building, which had been backfilled with a brickearth–clay deposit containing finds of a mid 16th-century date. Generally the pottery from Building 11 is typical 16th- and 17th-century forms and fabrics, equally divided between white Border wares and Post-medieval Redwares.

Open Area 12

(not illustrated)

Open Area 12 was represented by waterlain deposits, some of which may have predated the construction of Building 12. Due to the restricted nature of the investigations only two small areas of the deposit could be examined, making interpretation difficult. It is likely that some of the deposits included with Open Area 12 were contemporary with the use of Building 12. Pottery from these deposits was dated to the late 16th to early 17th century. A small number of horse bones, some butchered, and two dog bones were recovered and may be evidence of the animal-baiting on Bankside which is documented from the mid 16th century.

Building 12

(Figs 13, 14 and 15)

Building 12 was recorded in Evaluation Trenches E1 and E2. In E1 to the south (see Fig 2), three timber piles cut into waterlain deposits dated to the early 17th century (see Fig 14). One of the deposits, located to the north-west of the piles, contained dog bones. The piles may have been oak, with the highest at 1.50m OD. Further deposits of organic clays and silts had built up to the north, again some containing dog bones.

Directly above the position of the piles part of a vertical-sided robbing cut was recorded as being c 0.50m deep and over 0.90m wide (see Fig 15). The cut was elliptical, running north-west to south-east, and continued beyond the limits of the trench. The cut was flat bottomed and contained a dark brown silt with a number of bricks at its base. A second section of the robbing cut recorded further to the west also contained a brown silt with chalk fragments over broken bricks. The evidence points to the robbing of a brick and chalk wall foundation. The robbing was dated to 1640–60 by tobacco pipes found in the backfill.

Further evidence of Building 12 was recorded in Evaluation Trench E2 to the north, where there was no evidence of timber piles but a north-east to south-west robbing cut contained compacted brick rubble. The cut, whose depth was not established, was over 1.20m wide and continued beyond the trench limits. The rubble was partially overlain by a narrow east–west brick wall built over one of two decayed horizontally laid oak planks. The robbing cut underwent a slight change of alignment along its recorded length, and it was suggested by the excavator that the change in the angle of the foundation may have occurred at the location of the brick wall.

Building 12, although located in the two evaluation trenches, was not fully investigated and no attempt was made to retrieve samples from the piles for dendrochronological investigation. Subsequent archaeological work on the site did allow the reinvestigation of this area, as the piles were not under threat from the new development and it was agreed that they should be preserved *in situ*. The conclusions which can be reached from the limited evidence available are that the south-eastern part of the site was occupied in the 17th century by a large building constructed on timber piles. The alignment of the robbed wall foundation associated with the piles indicates that the building was multi-sided or elliptical in plan and approximately 16m in diameter. The found evidence suggests that it had 12 sides. Similar multi-sided structures have been found at the sites of the Rose theatre (Blatherwick 1998; Bowsher 1998; Bowsher & Blatherwick 1990) and the Globe theatre (Blatherwick & Gurr 1992; Blatherwick 1997; 1998).

Building 12 may be the remains of an animal-baiting arena, one of several which are known to have existed on Bankside from at least the mid 16th century. These buildings are shown on maps of the area as open structures built of brick and timber, with several galleries, and appear to have had thatched roofs. Kennels used to house dogs used in animal-baiting apparently lay nearby.

Deposits, one tentatively identified as a possible surface and some containing dog bones, lay to the north and west of the robbed foundations of Building 12 in what was presumably

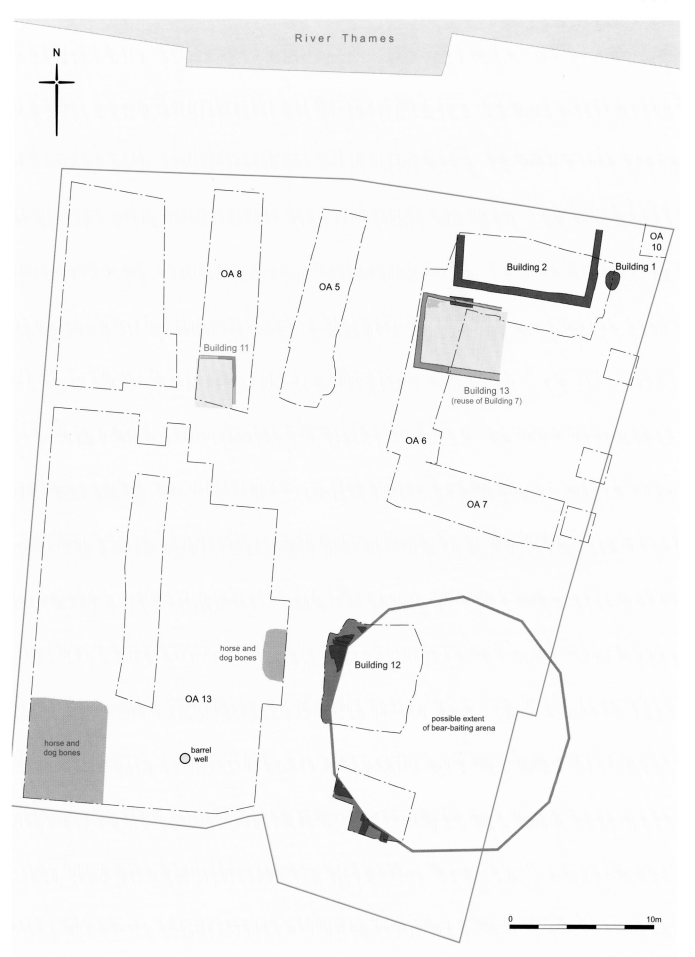

Fig 13 Principal archaeological features, Period 4: 16th and 17th centuries

Fig 14 Timber piles associated with the partially robbed wall line of Building 12, the possible animal-baiting arena, looking south-west. Scale 0.1m

Fig 15 Building 12 robbing cut and in situ timber piles, looking south-west. Scale 0.2m

an external area. The deposits were quite organic, suggesting that conditions were quite wet when they were formed.

The bone assemblage from these deposits was dominated by mature horse bones, with two-thirds showing butchery evidence, characteristic of dismemberment and filleting. Pathology, in the form of eburnation and a possible case of high ringbone characterised by bony expansion of the proximal end of the bone, and principally a complaint of heavy draught horses (Baker & Brothwell 1980, 120–2), was apparent on three horse phalanges, first noted during assessment (Ainsley 1998). These two factors, butchery and pathology, may be an indication that old workhorses were being brought into the site, from a knacker's yard, and perhaps used for food for the large number of dogs also recovered from this area.

Three dog bones were also recovered, two showing butchery marks. An ulna showed a series of transverse knife marks and a mature humerus had filleting evidence in the form of shaving on the bone resulting from defleshing. This butchery could indicate that the dogs themselves, when dead, were also used to feed other dogs.

A significant assemblage of dog and horse bones was also recovered from Open Area 13 to the west of Building 12, and these are discussed below.

The bulk of the pottery assemblage from Building 12 consists of typical 16th- and 17th-century types, dominated by locally produced redwares and white Border wares. There are also a number of noteworthy imports, which include German stonewares such as Frechen and Raeren, and also a range of wares from the Low Countries including Dutch redware and slipware. Additionally there are the remains of two Martincamp flasks, one a buff earthenware (MART 1), and the other a dark brown stoneware (MART 2).

The dating for Building 12 cannot be more precise than the 17th century, and most of this evidence came from the robbing of the foundation rather than from primary deposits. Also associated with the building were roof tiles, mostly peg tiles but also including pantiles, probable ridge tiles, and fragments of late 12th- to early 13th-century curved tiles.

Building 13

(Fig 13)

Building 13 represents the 17th-century reuse of the medieval chalk cellar of Building 7. The cellar walls were rendered with plaster and a brick floor laid (see Fig 8). The floor was covered by a thin deposit of hard, possibly vitrified ash. The cellar was subsequently infilled with a large amount of debris associated with tin-glazed ware (delftware) production. The cellar backfill also contained fragments of plaster and timber lathes derived from a timber building, and a small number of cattle and pig remains.

The large assemblage of tin-glazed ware waste from Building 13 included quantities of kiln furniture, biscuit-fired and glazed sherds. Documentary research shows Ferdinando Parkhurst was producing pottery from 1702 at Bear Gardens. Previously there have been no forms or decoration types that can be readily attributed to this pothouse, but the excavation of this kiln material has shed some light on the nature of the Bear Gardens' kiln's products (Fig 16). Clearly a large proportion of the forms are common to the late 17th or early 18th century. There is a paucity of glazed sherds, which is often the case with large groups of tin-glazed kiln waste. The few decorated sherds are commonly occurring types such as Chinese-inspired scenes or geometric or interlinked cable motifs <P9>. There are a number of plain-glazed sherds which include a small ointment pot <P10> (although this variety appears to be quite tall in relation to its diameter), a shallow version of an albarello-type storage jar <P11> and another mainstay of production – plain-glazed ware flat baseplates <P12>. Among the biscuit sherds there are a number of significant sherds which include a moulded fluted dish fragment <P13>, a pedestal-base salt cellar <P14>, an ornamental candlestick <P15> and the base of a cylindrical posset pot with pushed-out bosses <P16>. Additionally there is a porringer handle, with three heart-shaped holes and six lobes <P17>. On other similar sites there is a degree of uniformity regarding the pattern of porringer. Some patterns do occur on different sites but ultimately they are derived from different moulds. In all likelihood, barring the actual physical movement of moulds between factories, any extant porringer with a handle with three heart-shaped holes and six lobes will have been produced at Bear Gardens.

The assemblage sheds light on working practices and procedures. Tin-glazed ware was produced in two firings, the first being the biscuit firing, which was necessary to allow the glaze to 'fit' on to the body of the vessel, and avoid glaze crawling and giving an uneven finish. Clearly there was a large degree of waste produced after the biscuit phase, when vessels were discarded on account of either breakage or misfiring. There is slightly less waste post-glazing. The vessels were fired in saggars (earthenware containers) that protected the vessels from the direct effect of the heat. The saggar fragments recovered tend to come from cylindrical types, which have small triangular holes to accommodate pegs to support the vessels within the saggar. Two ointment pots <P18> and <P19> (see Fig 16) are coated in what appears to be either unfired or partially fired glaze. These vessels either were discarded prior to firing or failed to be fired sufficiently.

The presence of a small quantity of stoneware waste among the delftware waste confirms that stoneware was also made at the Bear Gardens kiln.

There was also evidence of other industrial activities taking place on the site at this time, with pits and deposits sealing earlier buildings and dated to the 16th century and later.

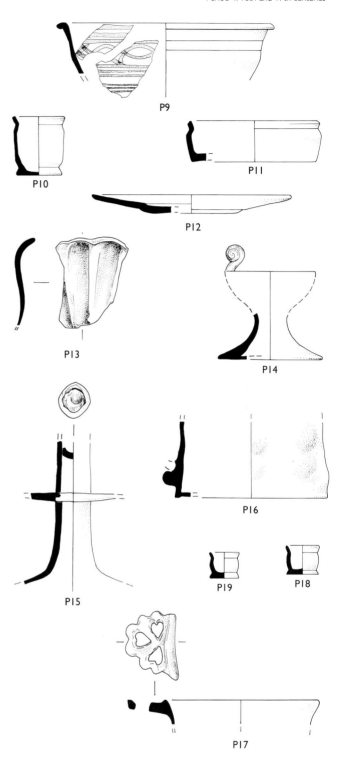

Fig 16 Post-medieval pottery <P9> – <P19>. Tin-glazed ware (delftware): bowl <P9>; ointment pots <P10><P18><P19>; albarello-type storage jar <P11>; plain-glazed flat baseplate <P12>; moulded fluted dish fragment <P13>; pedestal-base salt cellar <P14>; ornamental candlestick <P15>; cylindrical posset pot with pushed-out bosses <P16>; porringer handle <P17>. (Scale 1:4)

Open Area 5
(Fig 13)

Towards the north side of the site, Building 3 (see Fig 6) was sealed by layers of silt and debris, later cut into by several brick features, including drains and wells or soakaways. A large pit with vertical sides lay at the north end of the area and may have been related to numerous small postholes that cut into the highest surviving chalk floor surface of Building 3. It is not clear what the function of these postholes was. Similar small postholes were also noted in Evaluation Trench E3 (see Fig 2). The presence of sand and glass fragments in associated contexts suggests that they were somehow related to the glass industry. Open Area 5 is 17th century and later in date, comparable to deposits postdating Building 2.

Selected other finds from Open Area 5

STONE MORTAR

[349] <192> Caen stone (identified by Mark Samuel): rim and wall fragments of round, plain vessel with curving sides, h 150mm+, d 360mm; prominent tooling externally.

POSSIBLE BELL

[75] <19> Fragment of curved rod, d 33mm, wt 235g. ?Part of one of the integral top cannons from which a very large bell would have been suspended.

Open Area 6

(Fig 13)

External activity postdating Building 8 (see Fig 6) included several postholes of unknown function and sealed by clay dumps containing finds dating from the mid 14th to the late 16th century.

The dumps sealing Building 8 produced six fragments of a Raeren stoneware jug (near the modern border of Belgium and Germany) <P20> (Fig 17). This exceptional brown-glazed baluster jug has a minor frieze below the rim consisting of two figures in classical garb: one could be a a martial figure – he is wearing a flowing cloak and possibly holding a spear; the other is ?female – she is possibly holding a lotus flower in her outstretched hand. They are accompanied by groups of indistinct letters. On the shoulder of the jug, below this frieze, is an area of faceted incised diamond pattern. Below it is the main frieze, which has been applied as a separately moulded unit, and on one side has been partially detached and lost. The main frieze has a series of classical figures, including Themis (the goddess of order and justice): she is holding a sword and the scales of justice, although her eyes are not covered. The identification of the other figures remains problematic. To the right of Themis is a female figure holding a mirror – this is possibly a representation of truth, the mirror being the reflection of truth; or the mirror bearer is a handmaiden of Themis. To the left is another female figure, possibly dancing, and adjacent to her there appears to be a baby or possibly winged messenger, which may be supported by another figure now lost. The figures may be representations of the virtues – certainly justice is present, and possibly truth. There are small portions of script present: between Themis and the figure holding the mirror are the letters ZILL ..., and below the frieze is the word LEIDEN. One suggestion is that this is part of a motto rather than the city – *Leiden* is the German word for 'suffering' – and is perhaps an invocation concerned with illness and health.

Fig 17 Raeren stoneware jug with applied frieze of classical figures <P20> from external dump in OA6, Period 4

The word LEID[en] occurs on another panel jug from excavations in Southwark at New London Bridge House (site code NLB91). This example is substantially more complete. The theme of the frieze is the muses of the arts and sciences. In Greek mythology the muses were the nine daughters of Zeus and Mnemosyne (Memory). In late Roman times each daughter was associated with a specific art or science (such as epic poetry and astronomy). On the New London Bridge House jug the muses hold symbols to show which art or science they represent, and their names run along the top of the frieze. In addition to the muses there are other figures present, including the virtues TEMPERA[N]TIA and FORTITVDO – temperance and fortitude, and the remains of a figure holding scales, as in the Benbow House example. Possibly the latter jug had a similar mixture of muses and virtues.

The New London Bridge House example has at the bottom of the frieze the following inscription: ... MEI MISTER BAIDEM MENNICKIN POT ENBECKER ... IN LEID ... NO DVSENT 1579. Baidem Mennickin is known to have been producing elaborate moulded pieces south-west of Aachen; his surviving signed work spans 1575–85 (Gaimster 1997, 225).

A further example of a moulded panel jug has been excavated in Southwark from Morgan's Lane (Thompson *et al* 1998) and depicts nativity scenes, specifically the three kings bearing gifts and the flight into Egypt. Another similar frieze jug, this time a Westerwald jug depicting the seven liberal arts, was excavated from Magdalen Street (Chew & Pearce 1999, 26).

The presence of these elaborately decorated jugs on Bankside is significant, as they carried a high commercial and social premium and may have reflected the recreational function of the area at the time.

Open Area 7
(Fig 13)

Pits and cemented deposits, suggestive of industrial activity and dated to the 17th century, were recorded in Trench 3 sealing Building 6. A pit, context [394], contained horse remains which showed fairly extensive butchery, indicative of crude, rough meat processing, perhaps for the dogs that were used in baiting. In addition to the horse remains, only a small number of domesticates were recovered from Open Area 7, perhaps indicating that very little domestic activity was associated with this part of the site. A roe deer humerus is the only evidence of a wild species recovered from the site; it had a series of butchery marks indicative of filleting.

Open Area 7 also produced a moderate amount of tin-glaze waste sherds from the Bear Gardens kiln. These included a sherd from a saggar, sherds of manganese speckled purple and a sherd of plain white tin-glazed ware. The other sherds consisted of typical post-medieval sherds, with a small quantity of residual medieval pottery.

Open Area 8
(Fig 13)

Layers of demolition debris containing pottery of 15th- to 16th-century date sealed Building 4. In the southern part of the area there were several pits, one lined with clay and infilled with tile fragments, suggesting a possible industrial function.

The assemblage from Open Area 8 included important sherds, such as of a tin-glazed ware tankard with an imperfect discoloured glaze which may be a waster from the Bear Gardens kiln, a near intact Langerwehe or Raeren drinking jug, and an early Border ware cooking vessel which appears to have unfeasibly thin walls. Further evidence for money boxes on Bankside was identified in the form of a Green-glazed Border ware example with an unusual diagonal slit. Slits on Border ware examples are almost always vertical (Pearce 1992, 37) and it appears that in this case the slit was made in a rather cavalier fashion by the potter, rather than as a deliberate feature. The presence of a yellow-glazed Post-medieval Slip-coated Redware goblet with crenellated decoration <P21> (Fig 18), is another indication of the entertainment function of the Bankside area.

Selected other finds from Open Area 8
Key

[603] <210> Iron: bent rotary form, l 145mm, distorted kidney-shaped bow 41mm x 22mm, asymmetrical bit 25mm x 28mm with added outer side collared around narrowed stem (which has been narrowed further to accommodate this). The added outside part of the bit is presumably a repair following

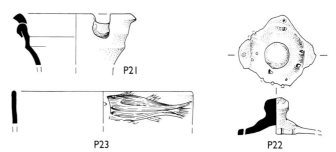

Fig 18 Post-medieval pottery <P21> – <P23>. Yellow-glazed Post-Medieval Slip-coated Redware goblet with crenellated decoration <P21>; Red Border ware lid with steam holes <P22>; polychrome Pearlware char dish <P23>. (Scale 1:4)

damage here to the original (it is ostensibly this addition which gives it the asymmetry).

Open Area 10
(Fig 13)

Chalk demolition debris containing finds of mid 16th-century date sealed Building 10 and was recorded in Pile Hole 9 at the extreme north-east corner of the site. Finds included another Green-glazed Border ware money box, as well as a near intact Raeren drinking jug, although overall the range of fabrics and forms was unremarkable.

Open Area 11
(not illustrated)

External activity recorded in Evaluation Trench E3 included numerous small postholes and pits. These features cut into the chalk demolition layer which sealed Building 2 and were overlaid by sandy deposits containing glassworking debris (see Figs 2 and 13). Similar deposits occured over most of the site and are evidence of the 17th-century glassworks at Bear Gardens. Generally, the evidence of glassworking was found in association with sandy deposits and recorded in the evaluation trenches (see chapter 3 below).

One of the Open Area 11 deposits also contained three horse bones from the lower leg and foot, one with pathology in the form of a small amount of extra bony growth, and three dog bones, all of which were badly eroded suggesting they were not *in situ* but redeposited. The remainder of the bone from these deposits derived from domesticates.

Noteworthy pottery from Open Area 11 is an elaborate Red Border ware lid <P22> (see Fig 18) with many steam holes. Lids are an uncommon type to be found in Red Border ware, and steam holes are not a standard feature. (Selected items of glass production and working are illustrated in chapter 3 below.)

Open Area 13
(Figs 13 and 19)

External activity was also recorded in the watching brief area in the south-western part of the site and surrounding Trench 5. Although deeply truncated by the foundations of a modern

31

building, this area produced a large amount of secondary material which may be associated with animal-baiting. Two dumps contained a total of 54 dog bones, many of which were entire, and 42 horse bones, again many whole. Two-thirds of the horse bones showed butchery, as did approximately one-fifth of the dog bones (see Fig 19).

The horse bones were all from mature animals, with an entire skull from a mature individual showing distinct wear on the anterior second premolar on both the left and right sides of the maxilla. Such wear has been noted on a number of archaeological horse mandibles, including three individuals from medieval contexts at LUD82 (1–6 Old Bailey/42–46 Ludgate Hill, EC4) (Rackham 1995b, 173), and has been attributed to the wearing of a bit (M Littauer in Clutton-Brock 1974, 93). The presence of this abnormal wear on second premolar teeth of a maxilla is not noted but could be related to a similar form of wear, possibly with an emphasis on the horse being pulled by reins rather than being controlled from behind, which would normally put strain on the mandible rather than the maxilla.

Butchery was common on the horse bones, but gnawing was not extensive. The butchery, indicative of defleshing, is suggestive of the bones being butchered and the meat fed to the dogs rather than whole bones being thrown for them to devour. It is possible that the dogs would be fed some bones with flesh remaining, but no such bones have been recovered. Not all butchery on horse bones resulted from defleshing, and some cut marks were more indicative of dismembering, with evidence of decapitation on one horse skull.

The dog bones recovered from Open Area 13 were mainly whole and from large, mature dogs. The proximity to the possible baiting arena, Building 12, may indicate that the bones were from dead fighting dogs butchered for their skin and meat. It seems likely that all of the dogs were being deposited in one area.

Although no direct dating evidence was recovered from the Open Area 13 dumps, it seems fairly certain that these bones are evidence of animal-baiting, which took place on Bankside from the mid 16th century until the building of the Hope playhouse in 1613. The Hope itself had a dual function of both staging plays and hosting blood sports, and soon reverted to being called the bear garden. Following the demolition of the Hope in 1656 there is evidence that animal-baiting with dogs continued on Bankside at Davies Bear Garden until 1682, when baiting moved north of the river (Blatherwick 1998).

Other features found in Open Area 13 included a well cut deep into the waterlain clays and constructed with two softwood casks, one above the other. The upper cask was c 1.40m high and 0.60m in diameter. It was not possible to record or recover any of the lower cask but it certainly continued below a depth of −2.0m OD. Of three staves from the upper cask examined by D M Goodburn, the most complete measured 1.385m long by 110mm wide by a maximum of 25mm thick. The other staves were of similar proportions although slightly thicker at 30mm. All had the distinctive groove ('croze') for the cask ends and an adjacent slight hollow

Fig 19 Some of the horse and dog skulls recovered from an external dump in OA13, to the west of the possible animal-baiting arena

('howel'). Both faces had clear saw marks, and the edges had been planed, although traces of wane were not removed along some edges. The insides were left unhollowed while the outside convex faces were only slightly rounded by shaving. All the staves were of a slow-grown knot-free softwood, probably pine.

Two small iron through nails were seen in the middle of the largest stave. These may have held some form of large washer or 'rove' in place on the outside, indicated by staining. Traces of roundwood hoops of hardwood were found adhering to the outside. All the staves were heavily charred on the outside, from the 'firing' used to heat the staves for bending.

The staves seem to derive from a cheaply made semi-tight cask of moderate quality and was perhaps used to contain loose goods. It is unlikely the cask contained liquid. The sawing rather than splitting of the staves and solidity of the timber suggest a post-medieval date. A dog skull and some peg tile were observed in the fill of the well but no datable material was recovered.

Period discussion

(Table 3)

The discovery of the remains of Building 12 is particularly significant, given its likely association with one of the Bankside animal-baiting arenas. Dating evidence from Building 12 and associated contexts indicates that it may be related to an arena rebuilt after the documented 1583 collapse. This is the first occasion that archaeological evidence of Southwark's animal-baiting arenas has been uncovered, and its location, against the southern edge of the bishop of Winchester's landholding, accords with the documentary evidence.

Building 12 may have been a 12-sided polygon with a diameter of *c* 16.0m (52ft 6in), smaller than the Rose playhouse (*c* 22.0m or 73ft) which was built some four years later. Although there is no evidence of the width of the galleries from which people would have watched a baiting, it would seem that the diameter of the baiting area itself would have been quite small – a surrounding gallery width of 3.0m (10ft) would only have allowed a baiting area of about 10m (33ft). This would have been both an intimidating and exhilarating arena in which to watch animals being baited and one in which the safety of the spectators could be regularly in doubt. The recovery of dog and horse bones – albeit from undated contexts – to the west of Building 12 may provide evidence of the documented pond for dead dogs, although evidence was not found of the pond itself.

If Building 12 is the post-1583 arena (subsequently owned by Edward Alleyn and Philip Henslowe) that was 'larger in Circuit and compasse', with galleries instead of the standings, it would be interesting to know its capacity. John Field, in his account of the collapse of William Payne's 'standings', estimated that there were a thousand people present (although exaggerating the number would have helped fuel his moral indignation), suggesting that the post-1583 arena would have held more than that. Henslowe's 1608 accounts for the bear gardens do, however, attest to its popularity in comparison with the Fortune playhouse.

Other significant Period 4 survivals include Building 2, whose secondary phase may indicate that it is the tenement rebuilt by Peter Street, although the recorded building is not the same size as that mentioned in Street's contract.

Overall, the nature of the Period 4 evidence from elsewhere on the site confirms the move towards industrial activity, and particularly glassworking and pottery manufacture.

2.5 Period 5: 18th and 19th centuries

Documentary evidence

Further evidence for the development of the Polsted lease comes from a lease dated 19 November 1776, when the property came into the hands of George Birch and John Mander (PRO CP/43/776). The Birch/Mander lease is briefly cited in Braines (1924, 94–5). It is worth detailing the evidence here, as it not only locates the first Bear Gardens foundry, in existence as early as 1748 and possibly earlier (see below), it also provides a guide to the location of the southern boundary of the bishop of Winchester's (and William Payne's) landholding. Braines cites the lease in eight different parts with all of part (ii) and some of parts (iii) and (vi) being located on the Benbow House site. The relevant parts of the precis of the Birch/Mander lease are as follows (Fig 20):

> ii) Four messuages on the bankside, bounded by a foundry and other premises, S. and W., the Bankside N., land of the bishop of Winchester E.

Table 3 Period 4 dating evidence (16th and 17th centuries)

Buildings 12 and 13; Open Areas 6 and 8				
activity	context	evidence	pot type	date range
Building 12	22	Ceramics	BORDG: -, FLDISH BORDY: -, DISH FREC: BOT, DJ MART 1: - MART 2: - PMR: - PMRE: JAR, PIP PMSR: PIP RAER: -	1550–1600
Building 13	515	Ceramics	BISC: ALB, BOWL, SAGG BORDG: - BORDY: FLDISH KILNF: - PMSRY: DISH TGW A: ALB, CHAR WANL, DISH, SAUC GEO	1630–1700
Building 13	516	Ceramics	BISC: ?BOT, BOWL, CHAR, CHP, CNDST ORN, DISH FLUT, JAR LG, JAR SM, JAR WD, LID, MUG, OINT, PORR, POSS, POSS CYL, SALT, TANK, TCUP KILNF: SAGG, SHELF LONS: - TGW: -, BOWL, CHAR BW, JAR LG, JAR SM, OINT – discoloured, PORR TGW A: BOWL CABL, JAR LG TGW B: handle TGW C: JAR, OINT, PLATE, PORR, SALT TGW D: CHAR CHIN, PORR CABL	1670–1705
Open Area 6	517	Ceramics	BORDG: -, PIP PMRE: MUG, PIP, PTCH PMSRG: GOB PMSRY: - RAER: JUG APDM TGW: BW Aldgate	1570–1600
Open Area 8	593	Ceramics	BORDG: -, BOX LANG: JUG PMRE: DISH, JUG, PIP PMSRY: DISH, JUG, GOB CREN, PIP RAER: DJ	1550–1600

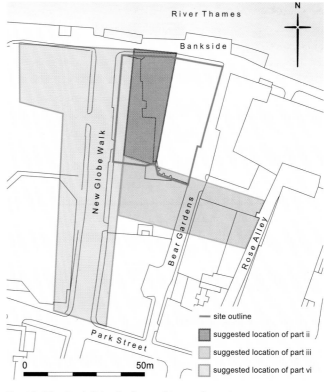

Fig 20 The Birch/Mander lease of November 1776. © Crown copyright. All rights reserved. Corporation of London LA 087254 00/03

iii) A dyehouse, a foundry (called the Bear Garden Foundry) with a tenement on the bankside adjoining (ii), and a smith's shop, all 'contiguous and adjoining to each other,' bounded by houses on the north side of Glasshouse Square, S., Black Lyon Court, the bishop's land, the four messuages and Bankside N., Rose Alley E., back part of houses on New Thames Street, W.

vi) The street called New Thames Street containing 39 messuages, two messuages on Bankside at the N. end of the street, the remaining part of the sheds called the Blast, and a mason's yard and shed, bounded by the colour shop and the lands of Bateman Lawley W., the Bankside N., Maid Lane S., Foundry, smith's shop and seven houses and sheds mentioned in (v) E.

In terms of locating industrial development on Bear Gardens, Braines (1924, 98) indicates that the Birch/Mander lease provides the location of the Bear Gardens glasshouses. In the 1776 lease there is apparently reference to a deed, dated 1750, which states that the glasshouses, mentioned in 1693, had been 'converted' into a smith's shop and foundry – in other words part (iii) of the Birch/Mander lease. Part (iii) of the lease extends on to the southern part of the Benbow House site. If there is mention of the location of the pothouse, Braines does not recount it. The Birch/Mander document also provides important information about the location of 'the Bear Garden Foundry' which was also located on part (iii) of the lease.

According to Saxby (1996, 14) the Bear Gardens foundry was established in 1780 by John Bradley. However, in the St Saviour's Poor Rate Book (for June 1748 to September 1766) there is an entry, dated June 1748, in which W Rawlinson is assessed for a foundry on Bear Gardens.

The location of Rawlinson's foundry is not certain although two factors point to it being on the west side of Bear Gardens, on the western half of part (iii) of the Birch/Mander lease. The first of these is the entry in the Poor Rate Book for June 1748. Assessments in the Poor Rate Book appear to indicate that the assessors worked along Bankside from west to east, taking in the streets and alleys (eg Thames Street, Bear Gardens etc) on the south side of Bankside as they went. This could imply that they initially assessed the west side of the streets and alleys, followed by the eastern sides and thus returning to Bankside. The entry, in 1748, for W Rawlinson is booked soon after the assessors appear to have entered Bear Gardens. The second factor is the wording of part (iii) of the Birch/Mander lease which describes that holding as including 'a foundry (called the Bear Garden Foundry) with a tenement on the bankside adjoining (ii)'. For the Bear Gardens foundry to have a tenement on Bankside adjoining part (ii) of the Birch/Mander lease, it must have been on the west side of Bear Gardens. It is, of course, conceivable that the foundry straddled the line of present-day Bear Gardens.

In November 1748 and June and November 1749, W Rawlinson was assessed with J Sunderland, but in June 1750 J Sunderland is assessed alone 'for Foundery' and this is the case

up to and including the assessment of July 1763. In October of that year Jhos Golding Esq & Co are assessed for the foundry, and in the February of 1764 J Goldney is assessed for a warehouse on the same premises. In July 1764 J Goldney Esq & Co are assessed for a foundry. Goldney continues to be assessed for a foundry up to and including the assessment of January 1771 (St Saviour's Poor Rate Book, February 1767 to July 1776) but in May of that year Alex Barclay appears to be assessed for the Goldney premises. Unfortunately there is no indication of Barclay's occupation or the function of the building he occupies but he continues to be assessed for the property up to and including the assessment of July 1776. Barclay does not appear in the Land Tax Assessment of 1775 or 1776 (St Saviour's Land Tax 1775 to 1794) although a 'warehouse', which appears to be located in the same place, is assessed as is a building in the occupation of 'Barclay and Phipps'.

The Land Tax Assessments of 1775 to 1794 can be confusing to use as they sometimes list the streets and alleys that run south from Bankside but on other occasions they do not. When they fail to list the streets and alleys to the south of Bankside they appear to include the properties that are known to be on those streets and alleys with the Bankside assessments.

The first appearance of a Bradley, previously thought to have established the Bear Gardens foundry (Saxby 1996, 14), is in the St Saviour's Land Tax Assessment for 1780. In this he is listed under Bankside. No value is placed on the assessment but 'pd' appears next to Bradley's name. Bradley appears on Bankside in 1781 and 1782 and Bradley and Co are assessed for a rent of three (presumably pounds) and are rated at eight shillings in 1783. This level of assessment continues through 1784 (Bradley & Co) and 1785 (Bradley & Son) but in 1786 John Bradley & Son are assessed, on Bankside, for a rent of sixty (?pounds) and a rate of £7 15s 0d. This could mean one of two things: either the Bradleys have moved to new premises on Bankside or they have massively expanded their holdings. Evidence from later Land Tax Assessments indicates that the larger premises are at the junction of Thames Street and Bankside – and so on the Benbow House site – but it is ambiguous concerning the location of the earlier assessed property. In 1787, Richard Bradley is assessed for the same property and continues to be so up to and including the 1794 Assessment. In the 1794 Assessment, Jas Bradley appears to be assessed for property at the north-east corner of Bear Gardens, possibly for the property shown to be in the possession of Mr Shears.

R Bradley is recorded as 'Founder' at 32 Bankside in the Universal British Directory of Trade and Commerce in 1790, and on the 1792–9 version of Richard Horwood's map (Fig 21) Mr Bradley's Foundry is shown on both the western and eastern sides of Bear Gardens. The foundry on the east side of Bear Gardens appears to relate to the eastern half of part (iii) of the Birch/Mander lease, while the foundry on the west side appears to occupy both the western half of part (iii) of the Birch/Mander lease and the bishop of Winchester's property.

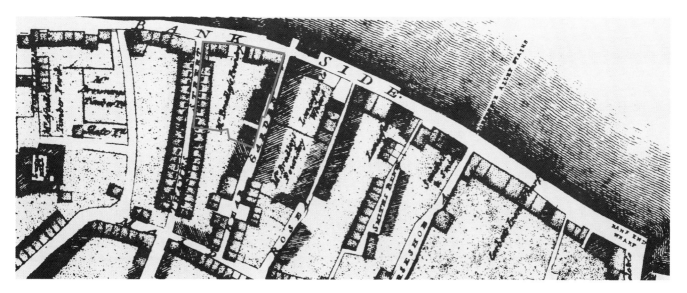

Fig 21 1792–9 version of Richard Horwood's map of Bankside

In the Post Office Annual Directory of 1803, J C and G Bradly *(sic)* are recorded as Brass & Iron Founders at 32 Bear-garden, Bankside, and by 1805 J Bradley occupied a foundry at 134 Maid-lane (Post Office Annual Directory 1805). The Maid-lane foundry is referred to as Eagle Foundry (Post Office Annual Directory 1811), and sometime between 1811 and 1817 was in the joint occupancy of John Bradley and James Benbow.

Around 1820 the Eagle Foundry appears to have moved to 32 Bankside and was occupied by John and Richard Bradley. Between 1835 and 1838 it came into the sole occupancy of James Benbow, with the foundry – according to Saxby (1996, 14) citing the London Directories (1780–1860) – lasting until around 1860. It would seem, though, that the foundry continued for much longer – as in the Post Office London Directory for 1883, James Benbow & Sons occupy the Eagle Iron Foundry at Bear Gardens and continue to do so until at least 1895.

Some indication of developments on the Benbow House site is provided by a 'Churchwardens Plan' discovered in the London Metropolitan Archives (P92/SAV/1276). Although the plan is undated it is bound within a folio which bears the inscription at the front 'Cleaned & Arranged by John Howe WGA [Warden of the Great Account] 1840' and shows premises held by Mr Shear and Messrs Bradley and Benbow on Bankside (Fig 22). At the bottom right-hand corner of the plan, it is marked 'C. F. Maltby, 34 Mark Lane, Clerk to No 2 Commtee of Assessors for St Saviour's Southwark' and a Key accompanies the plan indicating the 'Superficial Contents' of the mapped premises.

What the plan shows is that neither Mr Shears nor Messrs Bradley and Benbow have foundries on the Benbow House site but that they both have sheds, workshops, dwelling houses, open yards etc. The central and eastern part of Benbow House does not appear to be in the possession of either Mr Shears or Messrs Bradley and Benbow, and it is possible that this eastern piece of land

represents part (vi) of the Birch/Mander lease. It is possible that Bradley and Benbow's holding on the Benbow House site is equivalent to the western part (iii) of the Birch/Mander lease and the site of the original 1748 Bear Garden Foundry.

Evidence from the 1875 Ordnance Survey shows the eastern part of the Benbow House site occupied by an engineering works with the rest of the site occupied by yards and buildings. This is borne out by the Post Office London Directory of 1883 which locates Benbow's Iron Founders on Bear Gardens (presumably on the eastern side) and lists the other occupants on Bankside between Bear Gardens and Emerson (formerly Thames) Street.

Archaeological evidence

Period 5 produced extensive evidence of industrial activity, including an ironworks and foundry with several brick buildings.

Building 14
(Figs 23 and 24)

Brick walls forming the west, south and east sides of Building 14 were founded on the chalk walls of Building 7 to form a new building which measured at least 6.8m north–south and was *c* 4.0m wide. There was no evidence of a brick floor within the building, which contained *c* 0.25m of deposits. The lower part of this deposit was mixed yellow, white and red sands with fragments of glassworking (Fig 24), and the upper part a demolition dump of sand, ash, clinker and glass slag. The building was undoubtedly associated with the Bear Gardens glassworks.

Dating from Building 14 was limited to Post-medieval Redware (1600–1800) and some tobacco pipes (1730–60). Bricks dated to *c* 1450–1700 were also recovered from the building.

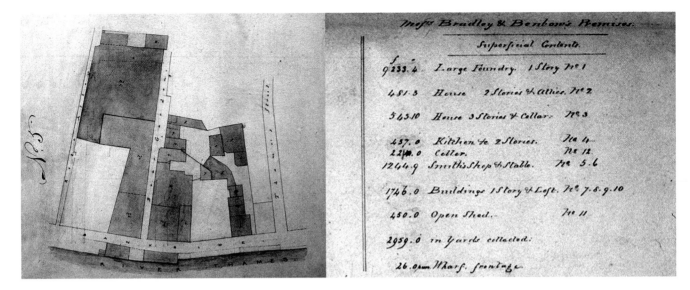

Fig 22 Undated churchwardens' plan of Shears, Messrs Bradley and Benbow premises on Bankside

Building 15

(Fig 23)

The evidence for Building 15 consisted of a series of brick walls, abutting the east wall of Building 16. The structure contained two phases. The first phase included two small rooms, both *c* 1.5m square (Rooms A and B). In the second phase another room also *c* 1.5m square was added (Room C) but with the walls at a slightly different alignment to those of the first phase. None of the rooms had brick floors and it is possible the building continued further to the south. The rooms were filled with deposits of fine sand and silt mixed with brick fragments. There were no glass fragments recovered from the building but it is probable that it had a function relating to both Buildings 14 and 16 – possibly as an ancillary building containing storerooms.

Building 15 postdated an Open Area 11 deposit which contained evidence of 17th-century glassworking. Dating for the building was otherwise limited to several fragments of 19th-century pottery from an upper demolition dump and tobacco pipes dated to 1820–40.

Building 16

(Fig 23)

Building 16 lay between Buildings 14 and 15 and comprised a north–south wall with an east–west return that abutted the south-east corner of Building 14. The building contained a yellow brick floor which was at least 6m long and 2.5m wide. In the south the floor was a mix of red and yellow bricks laid over an earlier floor of York slabs. A brick structure built into the floor was described as a slightly concave brick surface laid over a bed of tiles, and surrounded on three sides by scars where brick walls had once stood. The structure measured 1.20m north–south and over 1.0m east–west and may have been a hearth or furnace connected with metalworking. Overlying the floor was a deposit of yellow sand, but no metalworking fragments were recovered.

The reuse of the walls of Buildings 14 and 15 in the construction of Building 16 suggests that they may all have been part of one large building, although the use of yellow bricks suggests that Building 16 was part of a later phase. Building 16 also postdated an Open Area 11 deposit with evidence of 17th-century glassworking.

Selected other finds from Building 16

STRAP-END

[371] <167> Cast sleeved strap-end, 58mm x 34mm; dished-trefoil terminal with engraved floral motifs, engraved IHC (= Jesus) in black letter on sleeve; traces of gilding, and from ?leather strap, w 22mm, within sleeve. The flowers presumably allude to the Trinity; probably late 15th/early 16th century from the lettering; a number of similarly elaborate strap-ends also with the IHC motif are of similar date (*eg* Ward Perkins 1940, 270–1, fig 85, nos 1 and 2).

Building 17

(Fig 23)

Building 17 was an addition to the western side of Building 16 and was constructed of a similar mix of red and yellow bricks. The building measured 2.80m north–south and 2.0m east–west and was filled with brick rubble. No dating was recovered, but it was clearly a later phase associated with Building 16. A yellow and red brick base 1.25m x 1.0m was built outside and directly adjacent to the north-west corner of Building 17 and may have been the base for machinery. Building 17 also postdated an Open Area 11 deposit with evidence of 17th-century glassworking.

Building 18

(Fig 23)

Building 18 was constructed of red brick and lay to the north-west of Building 14. It measured at least 6.0m north–south and

River Thames

N

Building 20

Building 18

Building 21

A

B
Building 28

Building 14

drain

OA14

Building 22

Building 25

pit

drain

Building 23

OA15

drains

Building 17

Building 16

Building 24

Building 15

drain

furnace

Building 29

Building 26

0   10m

Fig 23 Principal archaeological features, Period 5: 18th and 19th centuries

Fig 24 Burnt sand deposits containing glassworking debris within Building 14, looking south. Scale 0.5m

over 4.0m east–west. The interior of the building was filled with brick rubble. A vaulted red brick drain running north–south lay just inside the west wall of the building and drained towards the north. Building 18 can be dated to the 18th century from its inclusion on the Horwood map of 1792–9, which shows the end of the building's south wall coinciding with the position of the next property to the east (see Fig 21).

Building 19

(not illustrated)

The corner of a red brick building predating Building 20 included walls which were observed to run at least 2.0m north–south and 2.0m east–west. The building was probably 18th century or earlier in date. The east wall of Building 19 lay 1.0m west of and parallel to the west wall of Building 18.

Building 20

(Figs 23 and 25)

Building 20 was a domestic building constructed of red brick and measured 8.0m east–west and over 9.0m north–south (Fig 25). The eastern external wall was built into small recesses cut in the west wall of Building 18 and must therefore have

postdated it. The layout of foundations suggests that Building 20 had six rooms, four of which had buttresses for fireplaces located along the central axis of the house. One of the smaller rooms had a brick floor with the remains of a brick wall that may have been for a staircase. A small brick structure in the corner of one of the rooms may have been associated with drainage. The rooms were infilled with brick rubble deposits.

Building 20 does not appear on the Horwood map of 1792–9 (see Fig 21) and is therefore probably 19th century in date. Bricks from the walls are late 17th century or later. Pottery recovered from the rubble is early to mid 19th century and may indicate a date of construction rather than demolition. Building 20 appears on the Ordnance Survey map of 1863 as two properties.

Building 21

(Fig 23)

Building 21 lay just to the west of Building 20, the gap between the two buildings measuring c 0.80m and occupied by a vaulted brick drain. Building 21 measured over 7.0m north–south and over 3.0m east–west, the north and west sides lying beyond the limits of excavation. The east and south walls of the building were constructed of red brick. Associated with these walls was a brick floor which was only 1.60m wide and stopped abruptly. A scar on this floor suggested the location of an internal wall, one brick wide, parallel to the outer wall. Building 21 appears on the Horwood map of 1792–9 as a very narrow building (see Fig 21), with the edge of the brick floor coinciding with the start of another property.

Building 22

(Fig 23)

Brick Building 22 abutted the south wall of Building 21 and measured 3.20m north–south and 2.40m east–west. The building enclosed the remains of a cobbled surface. It was not clear if this was an internal or external surface. Access to Building 22 may have been through the gap between Buildings 20 and 21. Building 22 was 18th century in date and postdated the construction of Building 21.

Building 23

(Fig 23)

Building 23 was a brick building situated to the south of Building 20 and measuring 4.80m north–south and 3.60m east–west. The south wall of the building also formed part of the north wall of Building 24 to the south.

Building 24

(Fig 23)

Building 24 was another brick building, only the eastern part of whose plan was recovered on site, the rest coming from the Ordnance Survey map of 1863. The building measured c 9.0m east–west and 4.0m north–south. Both Buildings 23 and 24 cut into an Open Area 11 deposit of silt and charcoal which contained evidence of earlier glassworking.

Buildings 23 and 24 are 19th century in date as they are not on the Horwood map of 1792–9, but appear on the Ordnance Survey map of 1863. Only residual pottery was recovered from within the walls of Building 23.

Building 25
(Figs 23 and 26)

Building 25 was a small brick building located at the north-east corner of Building 23. It measured 2.40m north–south and 2.0m east–west, the walls enclosing an oval brick-lined pit or tank that was 0.85m deep and which did not have a floor. The structure probably had an industrial function. It was backfilled with a rubble deposit and still held water.

The relationship between Buildings 25 and 23 is unclear. Although recorded as cutting through Building 23, the pottery recovered from the backfill is of late 18th-century date. Building 25 may predate Buildings 23 and 24; it does not appear on the Horwood map of 1792–9 or on the OS map of 1863.

To the north, between Buildings 20 and 25, was an external area (Open Area 14) with a brick floor surface and a shallow brick drain which may have been contemporary with Building 25.

The late 18th-century ceramics from the Building 25 pit or tank include a polychrome Pearlware straight-sided dish decorated with a fish <P23> (see Figs 18 and 26). This is a char dish, char being a freshwater fish that was made into a paste and served in the vessel. Char vessels were produced in tin-glazed ware, creamware, whitewares and pearlware (Austin 1994, 201).

Fig 25 The ground plan of Building 20, looking north (with walls of Buildings 17, 18, 21, 23 and 25 visible around it). Scale 1.0m

Fig 26 The Pearlware char dish <P23> and the Transfer-printed nursery cup <P24>, both from the brick tank in Building 25

Fig 27 Building 26 to the right, looking east, with concrete pile caps and backfilled evaluation trench to the left. Scale 1.0m

With the char dish was a Transfer-printed ware cup <P24> (see Fig 26), a nursery cup inscribed with 'A PRESENT FOR A GOOD GIRL' and accompanied by a vignette of a figure of a woman standing next to a London milestone, adjacent to which is a male figure holding an accidentally discharging gun that appears to have shot another man in the backside! Whether this is a moralistic tale or a representation of a contemporary event is not known.

Although bricks of late 17th-century date or later were associated with Building 25, the presence of a possible shallow frog in one brick suggests an 18th-century or later date.

Building 26

(Figs 23 and 27)

Building 26 lay in the extreme south-east corner of the site and was a well-built brick structure measuring 5.0m north–south and at least 11m east–west. Within the main walls of the building were a series of brick walls forming small bays, round the top of which were traces of floors of sandstone slabs and brick. The bays were infilled with a mix of fragments of charcoal, coal and brick rubble. It was not possible to establish

whether these bays had floors. The ground plan of the building may indicate that it was composed of small rooms or bays used for storage (see Fig 27). Building 26 may be early to mid 18th century in date as it cuts through 17th-century glasshouse deposits and may be one of the buildings on the Horwood map of 1792–9 (see Fig 21). It should be noted that there is a correlation between the location of this building and area (iii) on the 1776 Birch/Mander lease (see Fig 20) which lists among other things a dyehouse.

One of the internal walls of Building 26 was constructed of reused bricks dated to *c* 1450–1700. The outer wall of the building had late 17th-century or later bricks. No other dating evidence was recovered.

Building 27

(not illustrated)

Building 27 was recorded in Evaluation Trench E3 (see Fig 2) and consisted of a corner and brick walls extending 2.0m north–south and over 2.0m east–west. The building was built on Bankside facing the river and continued to the north and to the east beyond the excavation area. Little can be said about the building due to the high amount of truncation caused by Building 28, but it was probably late 17th or 18th century in date.

Building 28

(Fig 23)

Building 28 was also recorded in Evaluation Trench E3 and may have replaced Building 27. There were four phases of construction associated with Building 28.

Building 28 phase 1 measured 5.0m east–west and over 7.0m north–south, with poorly built brick walls which incorporated some fragments of chalk and stone that had probably been reused from the underlying medieval Building 2.

Building 28 phase 2 consisted of a rebuild with the walls doubled in thickness and an internal east–west wall creating two rooms (Rooms A and B). A step led down to the northern Room A, while the southern Room B had a tile floor. Located further to the south was either another room or, perhaps more likely, an external area. The external eastern wall of the building was modified by the addition of a small vaulted brick cellar, possibly for storage of coal. This addition may have been contemporary with the addition of a curved brick wall set on planking and associated with a cesspit or tank.

Building 28 phase 3 consisted of the replacement of the tile floor in Room B with a thin concrete floor and the rendering of its walls with white plaster. The west wall had traces of a shelf and along the eastern side of the room a raised brick structure with an oval drain led to an outlet pipe which drained to the north through a hole in the wall. These may have been part of a working surface with a sink, suggesting the final use of this building was as a scullery.

Building 28 phase 4 represents the final phase in the history of the building and includes the construction, to the south, of a number of brick drains and two circular pits or wells, perhaps relating to an industrial activity. Building 28 can be dated to the 18th or early 19th century.

Building 29
(Figs 23 and 28)

Building 29 included several phases of construction but the lack of full excavation made their individual identification impossible. The building comprised several brick walls surrounding cobbled surfaces, one with a brick sump. To the south there was a brick floor in an internal area. The surfaces where sealed by a hard deposit of iron waste. Iron waste deposits were also found scattered over the southern part of the site, suggesting the ironworking activity was located mainly in this area.

Adjacent to the north-west corner of Building 29 a brick structure formed the base of a furnace (see Fig 28). The structure measured 2.20m north–south and 2.0m east–west, with the top of the structure missing. It comprised two chambers, of which the eastern was oval with a curved floor and was 0.80m wide (the full length was not seen). To either side were thick brick walls. The western chamber, which was rectangular with a curved floor and was 0.50m wide, formed a stokehole. Between the chambers was a narrow slot that would originally have held an iron door. The structure appears to have been a reverberatory furnace, which functioned by reflecting heat off a curved roof on to the metal.

A nearby pit contained numerous iron and copper-alloy studs, buckles and other metalwork, presumably discarded products from this furnace. Evidence of both copper-alloy and iron buckles in a variety of forms and sizes, many of them very small and still joined from casting, comprised hundreds of individual accessories. The circumstances under which these were discarded is unclear but they are presumably 19th-century factory stock.

A brick drain and sump to the north-west of Building 29 and the furnace area may have been associated with it and was infilled with industrial debris.

Building 29 can be dated to the late 18th century when there was a foundry on Bear Gardens run by the Bradley family and later by James Benbow. The foundry continued in operation as late as 1895.

Selected other finds from Building 29

COPPER-ALLOY OBJECTS

[77] <15> Double-oval frame.

[38] <47> Group of c 150 (eight layers of four rows of four) rectangular frames with central bars each holding a pair of pins; stack originally held together with iron wire.

[236] <161> Over 200 (several stacked) – similar form to preceding items.

[236] <163> Over 100 (includes large stack) rectangular frames with pairs of pins (?studs attached).

[236] <296> Rectangular frame.

[236] <306–9> Tens of rectangular frames – at least four varieties, including ones with pairs of pins on the frame and on central bars.

IRON OBJECTS

[77] <17> Group of 100+ (?six layers of four rows of four) rectangular frames with central bars each holding a pair of pins.

[236] <160> Tens (a few are stacked) of rectangular frames with pairs of pins on the frame and on central bars (some may be copper alloy obscured by rust).

[236] <162> Eight rectangular frames with double pins on central bars (large size).

Fig 28 The partially exposed furnace to the north of Building 29, looking south-east. Scale 1.0m

Table 4 Period 5 dating evidence (18th and 19th centuries)

Building 25 activity	context	evidence	pot type	date range
Building 25	407	Ceramics	CHPO ROSE: SAUC ENMD	1780–1800
			CREA: CHP, WSTL	
			LONS: BLACKP, JUG	
			PEAR: POLY DISH FISH	
			PEAR BW: CUP FLOR, LID TPOT,	
			SAUC CHIN, SAUC FLOR	
			PMR: BOWL, JUG	
			RBOR: CHP	
			RESTG: TANK	
			SWSG SCRB: CHP, TANK	
			TPW: CUP, CUP LAND, SAUC	
			WILL	

[236] <304> Tens of similar form to preceding (medium size).
[236] <305> About 20 of similar form to preceding (small size).

Open Area 15
(Fig 23)

Open Area 15 lay to the east of Buildings 14, 15 and 16, and contained two large brick drains. One of the drains contained evidence of metalworking. Both drains entered a third drain that ran towards the north-east, presumably to a sewer located under Bear Gardens. It is impossible to say which buildings the drains relate to, but taken with the concentration of drains cutting through Building 28, this part of the site may be considered external. Certainly all the drains are leading eastwards away from the site and under the adjacent road, Bear Gardens.

Period discussion
(Table 4)

The documentary and archaeological evidence for Period 5 points to the increased industrialisation of the site, with the recorded buildings appearing to be concentrated on the bishop of Winchester's land. It is difficult to ascribe original functions to the recorded buildings and the suggestion that Building 14 was associated with the glassworks does not tie in with the assessment of the documentary evidence. It is conceivable that the material recovered from Building 14 was dumped there after the glassworks (to the south?) went out of use.

Positive identification of some of the buildings is provided by the churchwardens' plan (see Fig 22), with Buildings 14, 17, 20, 23, 24, 26, 28 and 29 appearing to be identifiable. Evidence from the plan suggests that both the Shear and the Bradley and Benbow foundries were located to the east of Bear Gardens and that the Benbow House site held ancillary buildings such as houses, kitchens, workshops and open yards.

3

Glass production and glassworking evidence

Geoff Egan

The colourless ('crystal' – actually slightly greyish) and green glassmaking/working evidence makes up a sizeable assemblage from the Benbow House site. This, along with the blue fragments, presumably all derives from one or more of the manifestations between 1671 and 1726 (and possibly later) of the historically attested Bear Gardens glass factory. Window glass was certainly produced here, but it is difficult to define for certain any range of vessels that may have been manufactured. Only one vessel fragment appears seriously distorted (G57, which is of a form and colour combination that is not otherwise represented in the assemblage) – it is always possible this could have been heat-damaged elsewhere than at its place of manufacture. There are also some moils (accumulations of glass around the mouth of the inflating iron) (G50–1, G53 and G55–6) and two unstratified, tubular pieces of blowing waste (G54 Fig 29), but the majority of pieces are open to interpretation as used vessels or window glass, and they may possibly include cullet for recycling collected from many sources. None of this material is in primary association with any processing structure. Despite this, overall the assemblage unmistakably derives from a production site. While the commoner vessels present (whether or not these were actually products) are readily and widely paralleled, it is very difficult to find any comparable items for the finest of the pieces recovered, particularly those in blue, either among excavated material or in collections. Dating, both in broad terms from some of the vessel fragments themselves and from other associated finds of ceramics and clay tobacco pipes, suggests two phases – late 17th century to *c* 1680 and *c* 1690 to early 18th century – from an enterprise which according to historical sources lasted over half a century under various different owners.

Several specific vessel forms, notably plain and decoratively moulded beakers and plain bottles, are represented among the colourless and blue pieces retrieved, and there are also some (possibly stemmed) cups, and two fragments of plates – one colourless and another in blue (G96 Fig 30 and G111 Fig 33) – two bases from lamps (an unusual category in glass at this date, G97–8 Fig 30) and a (possible) handled pot (G99 Fig 30). The majority of these finds come from context [10] in Open Area 11, which produced clay pipe dates up to *c* 1680. A single blue piece, G109 (Fig 33), has a white trail, and G112 (Fig 33) is shaped from an accomplished mould. Many of the colourless and blue vessel fragments can be characterised as extremely delicate, fine wares from their very thin walls and exceptionally even, blemish-free metal – these products were probably among the best available in London at the time. There is no definable blue waste (G111 Fig 33 and G116 Fig 31 are perhaps only slightly distorted) and so it remains an open question whether or not any of these vessels were made at the factory (the relatively small proportion of fragments of this colour may well reflect a small-scale, non-wasteful sideline at whatever factory/factories they actually came from). A couple of the amorphous waste pieces are slightly purplish (G17 and G30, cf G48) and another is brownish (G23) – these may all be colourless glass accidentally tinged from impurities and

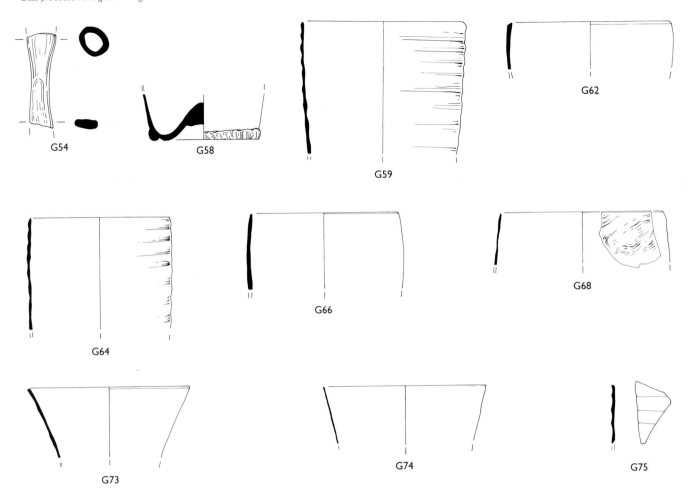

Fig 29 Post-medieval glass 1. (Scale 1:2)

discarded for this reason. Thick sheets of colourless plate glass (G127ff) could be for prestigious windows or mirrors. One of these fragments has an engraved inscription (G130 Fig 34) and another piece of window glass has engraved lines (G138 Fig 34). The green glass seems primarily to have been for small 'steeple' bottles (G117ff – not necessarily products of the factory) and windows – some crown-glass edge pieces and fragment G144 with a central bullseye are (if not from accidental breakages) evidence for cutting at the site.

Also found were several pieces of sizeable crucibles (G153ff), each of which would have weighed several kilos (no complete profile was retrieved). No *in situ* plant was uncovered during the limited fieldwork, but the concentration of waste suggests that the factory was extremely close – structural evidence could perhaps survive in the immediately underlying deposits that were not in the brief to investigate. There is some possibility of confusing furnace fragments and unfamiliar categories of waste from glassworking with those from the earlier tin-glazed ware manufacture (which was certainly present as recognisable waste on the site) and perhaps from other industries.

The Bear Gardens factory is fairly obscure in historical terms (it is not mentioned in Godfrey's 1975 book, which only goes up to 1640) and it has never been considered outside a very specialised literature. Its modest

claim to fame in some circles hitherto was as the 'originator' of crown glass – patently untrue (see Frank 1982, 25, and many finds at medieval monastic sites – Egan in prep a; in prep b – though crown pieces are indeed among those recovered in the present assemblage). A 19th-century commentator suggested it was the first maker of a 'light sky-blue' version of crown glass (Noël Hume 1995, 32) – a source for this late tradition can perhaps be read into some of the recovered bluish-green crown fragments, like G141–6 and G150. The factory was in the hands of a syndicate of plate-glass manufacturers in the latest phase, from *c* 1691, and, as noted, plate glass is correspondingly present among the finds.

The archaeological evidence is a significant new source of information, with the potential to make this little-known enterprise and its products more widely appreciated. This is the first detailed account of excavated industrial evidence for any of the early factories of London – the main location in England for this industry. A more extensive group of crystal waste found at a site just outside the City walls at Aldgate (AL74) and a smaller group from a site at Broad Street (BRO90) researched by John Shepherd, are both thought to be from Robert Mansell's early 17th-century Gracechurch Street enterprise, and have still to be fully published.

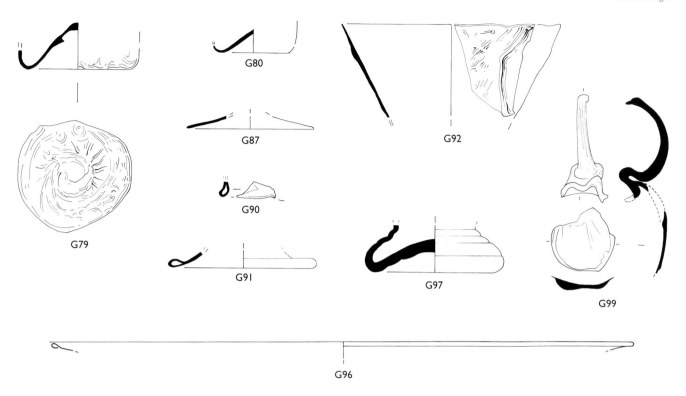

Fig 30 Post-medieval glass 2. (Scale 1:2)

GLASS CATALOGUE

B	building	h	height	OA	open area	w	width	?	uncertain
d	diameter	L	length	th	thickness	wt	weight	??	very uncertain

Tank/pot metal

Comprises approximately 10.25kg (c 2.5kg of which is stratified).

Colourless

G10 [7] <75> OA11
Amorphous spillage (slight greenish tinge); wt 231g.

G11 [75] <137> OA11
Plano-convex fragment incorporating bubbles and pieces of dirt (solidified partly over edge of flat surface); wt 65g. (See G18.)

Green

G12 [44] <259> OA11
Amorphous lumps; wt 74g.

G13 [76] <90> OA11
Amorphous masses and trails; wt 84g.

G14 [329] <191> OA11
Bluish-green: variety of amorphous masses; wt 790g.

G15 [329] <322> OA11
Four bluish-green fragments; wt 58g. ?Possibly from distorted vessels.

G16 [500] <189> B14
Amorphous masses with some trails (includes one with latter fused on to former); wt 475g.

G17 [500] <267> B14
Amorphous, discrete pale green and purplish masses fused together; wt 3.7g.

G18 [500] <270> B14
Amorphous masses (together unsorted with colourless ones); wt 3.7kg.

G19 [507] <188> B14
Amorphous masses; wt 455g.

G20 [507] <242> B14
Amorphous mass attached to pinkish stone –

heat-altered Reigate stone (identified by Ian Betts); wt 271g. The stone may well be from the furnace structure.

G21 [509] <185> B14
Two amorphous masses, one slightly bluish; wt 18g.

G22 [unstratified] <112>
Mainly pale green, but some colourless and slaggy opaque material; wt 7.745kg.

Brown

G23 [329] <262> OA11
Amorphous mass; wt 19g. ?Iron-stained.

Runnels etc

Fragments showing evidence of having been pulled out/trailed.

Comprises *c* 1.9kg (of which 0.9kg is unstratified).

Colourless

G24 [44] <184> OA11
Amorphous masses and trails; wt 44g.

G25 [54/55] <182> OA11
Amorphous masses and trails; wt 27g.

G26 [329] <261> OA11
Irregular rod: surviving l 85mm, max d 21mm; wt 51g.

G27 [500] <247> B14
Amorphous trails; wt 17g.

G28 [500] <273> B14
Amorphous trails; wt 5g.

G29 [500] <274> B14
Irregular ?droplet fragment; wt *c* 1g.

G30 [507] <244> B14
Amorphous purplish trail; wt 29g.

G31 [507] <321> B14
Amorphous trail; wt 30g.

G32 [unstratified] <311>
Amorphous trail; wt 3.2g.

Green

G33 [10] <58> OA11
Circular trail: d *c* 17mm, possibly broken off a vessel; wt 1g.

G34 [54/55] <249> OA11
Amorphous lumps and trails; wt 14g.

G35 [75] <113> OA11
Amorphous trails; wt 82g.

G36 [75] <114> OA11
Amorphous masses with some trails; wt 590g.

G37 [75] <183> OA11
Amorphous trail; wt 1.9g.

G38 [248] <257> OA11
Amorphous, twisted trail; wt 8.6g.

G39 [507] <243> B14
Amorphous trail with two transverse splits (?blade cuts) in side; wt 53g.

G40 [unstratified] <100> (Fig 32)
Massive pale green lump with multiple thread-like trails on upper surface; wt 870g. This was presumably located so that it repeatedly received filaments from molten glass passed over it.

G41 [unstratified] <116>
Amorphous pale bluish-green trails; wt 34g.

Slag

Approximately 9kg appears to relate to the glass industry.

G42 [10] <–> OA11
5kg attached to base of white-fired base of crucible for glass.

G43 [44] <260> OA11
Glassy – range with zoning from vesicular to solid, blackish to mid green (all opaque); wt 3.1g.

G44 [329] <250> OA11
Wt 1.115kg.

G45 [407] <181> B25
Amorphous, opaque mid green (khaki), glassy masses, with vesicular zones; wt 1.915kg. Presumably connected with the glass industry, even though no other glass material was recognised from this context.

G46 [500] <246> B14
Opaque green, glassy and vesicular; wt 3.2g.

G47 [507] <241> B14
Mixed translucent green glass to opaque grey, with some superficial yellow material; wt 152g.

In addition to the pieces described above, there is 1.4kg of brown, vesicular slag from context [500] and 2.91kg from context [507]; these may be from a different industry, despite their discovery alongside definite glass waste.

A 4.125kg heterogeneous, vesicular whitish-grey and dark reddish-brown lump <202> from context [516] is probably also unrelated – no other glassworking material came from this deposit (though there is a base fragment of a very large, dark green glass carboy).

Droplets (neat, fire-rounded)

Colourless

G48 [44] <314> OA11 (Fig 32)
Two (one purplish); wt 6g.

G49 [54/55] <315> OA11 (Fig 32)
Wt 2.7g.

Blowing waste

Pieces broken, following the blowing of vessels, from inflating irons. Comprises <60g.

Colourless

G50 [44] <327> OA11
Moil fragment: d internally *c* 30mm, externally *c* 45mm; wt 11g.

G51 [54/55] <316> OA11
Moil fragment in form of curved strip: d internally *c* 12mm, externally *c* 25mm; wt 6.7g.

G52 [93] <130> OA11 (Fig 32)
Joining, translucent, streaked medium green and paler bluish/greyish-green fragments, making almost an eighth of a sphere: d 50mm; wt 9.9g.

This (within the assemblage) uniquely coloured item is likely to be waste material from the inflation of material presumably discarded promptly because of its unsuitable hue (suggestion by John Shepherd).

G53 [unstratified] <118>
Moil fragment; wt 3.3g.

G54 [unstratified] <103> (Fig 29)
Two tubes, broken off at each end, flattened by a tool at one end and flaring towards the other; l 46mm and 52mm; wt 20g.

Bluish-green

G55 [7] <74> OA11 (Fig 32)
Ring-pontil moil: internal d *c* 20mm, external *c* 40mm; wt 16g.

G56 [unstratified] <317>
Moil fragment: internal *c* 25mm, flaring externally to d *c* 60mm+; wt 12g.

Distorted vessel fragment

There seems to be only one definite waster in this sense (G90 and G113 have minor faults that might not have affected the saleability of the complete vessels). Comprises >5g.

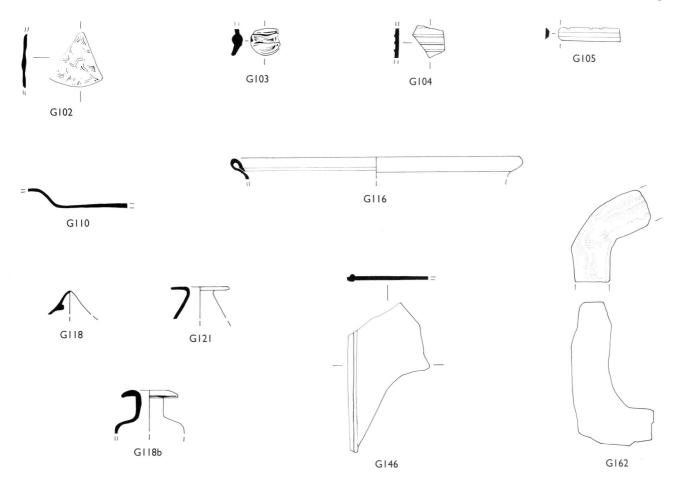

G102

G103

G104

G105

G110

G116

G118

G121

G118b

G146

G162

Fig 31 Post-medieval glass 3. (Scale 1:2)

Colourless

G57 [10] <43> OA11
?Pushed-in base: d approx 70mm+,
with distorting fold; wt 5.1g.
Possibly from a cup, or more likely a
bottle (rather than an off-centred alembic
head).

Other vessel fragments

Colourless

beakers (stemless drinking vessels)
G58 [10] <1> OA11 (Fig 29)
Pushed-in base: d 60mm, with part of plain
wall; applied, milled trail.

G59 [10] <2> OA11 (Fig 29)
Fragments of at least two vertical rims and
pieces of walling: d *c* 85mm, all with
horizontal ribbing.

G60 [10] <4> OA11
Plain, outwardly bevelled vertical rim:
d *c* 90mm.

G61 [10] <5> OA11
As preceding item (thicker wall).

G62 [10] <12> OA11 (Fig 29)
As preceding item (possibly part of same vessel).

G63 [10] <13> OA11
Plain, vertical rim: d 80mm.

G64 [10] <14> OA11 (Fig 29)
Plain rim: d 90mm, with moulded horizontal
ribbing.

G65 [10] <32> OA11
Base: d *c* 70mm, with milled trail.

G66 [10] <33> OA11 (Fig 29)
Fragment of plain, vertical rim: d 85mm.

G67 [10] <34> OA11
Plain, vertical rim: d *c* 90mm.

G68 [10] <36> OA11 (Fig 29)
Vertical rim with moulded spiral ribbing:
d *c* 80mm.

G69 [10] <37> OA11
Plain, vertical rim: d *c* 80mm.

G70 [10] <38> OA11
Plain, vertical rim: d *c* 80mm.

G71 [10] <42> OA11
Plain, vertical rim: d *c* 80mm.

G72 [10] <55> OA11
Plain vertical rim with horizontal ribbing:
d *c* 90mm.

G73 [10] <56> OA11 (Fig 29)
Plain, flared rim: d *c* 90mm, with slight
horizontal ribbing.

G74 [10] <84> OA11 (Fig 29)
Plain, very thin vertical rim:
d *c* 95mm.

G75 [10] <89> OA11 (Fig 29)
Wall fragment: d *c* 80mm, with four surviving
ribs horizontally.

G76 [10] <93> OA11
Plain rim fragment with horizontal ribbing:
d *c* 80mm.

G77 [10] <96> OA11
Plain, thin vertical rim: d *c* 90mm.

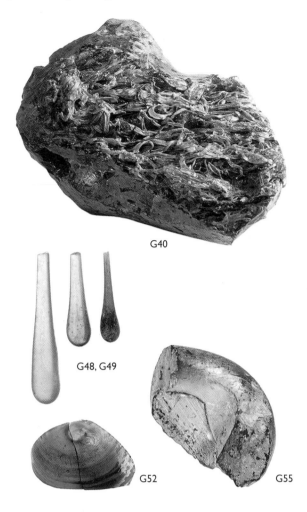

G40

G48, G49

G52

G55

Fig 32 Post-medieval glass 4

G78 [10] <325> OA11
Two walling fragments: d *c* 75mm and 80mm, moulded with horizontal ribbing. Presumably from beakers.

bottles

PUSHED-IN BASES
G79 [10] <26> OA11 (Fig 30)
D *c* 75mm+; moulded with rays surrounded by two rings of pellets.

G80 [10] <27, 79–82> OA11 (Fig 30 of <80>)
D *c* 17mm+ – 23mm+.

PLAIN, HORIZONTAL RIM
G81 [10] <24> OA11
Fragment: d *c* 38mm.

cups

BASES
G82 [10] <44> OA11
Flattish: d *c* 90mm.

G83 [10] <45> OA11
As preceding item: d *c* 70mm.

G84 [10] <46> OA11
As preceding item.

G85 [10] <57> OA11
As preceding item: d *c* 90mm.

G86 [10] <59> OA11
As preceding item: d *c* 80mm.

G87 [10] <86> OA11 (Fig 30)
Flattish base, with slight change in angle: d *c* 70mm.

G88 [10] <89> OA11
Flattish base: d 80mm.

G89 [10] <92> OA11
Flattish base: d *c* 70mm.

G90 [500] <279> B14 (Fig 30)
Fragment of folded basal rim: d ?*c* 80mm; fold distorted; wt 0.5g.
?From a cup.

G91 [549] <234> OA8 (Fig 30)
Fragment of pushed-in base folded at rim: d *c* 85mm+.

RIM
G92 [10] <35> OA11 (Fig 30)
Flaring, slightly waved rim: d *c* 100mm, moulded with ?arched frame and vertical row of 'chequers'.

WALLING
G93 [10] <95> OA11
Round fragment.

G94 [248] <255> OA11
Plain fragment.

G95 [500] <303> B14
Several plain fragments.

plate

G96 [10] <87> OA11 (Fig 30). Several edge fragments, folded at rim: d *c* 300mm.

lamps

These would have had a stem and an upper well to hold the wick in the oil; the thick bases gave stability. (Identified by John Shepherd.)

G97 [10] <6> OA11 (Fig 30)
Slightly brownish, thick, pushed-in base: d 80mm, with concentric moulding, folded over and triply rebated to ?vertical wall.

G98 [10] <132> OA11 Fragment of base as preceding item (colour is usual greyish).

handled pot

G99 [10] <50> OA11 (Fig 30)
(Three pieces) fragment of thin vessel wall joined to applied 'claw' in form of folded-over pad, which continues as curved, tapering hollow handle. ?From a posset pot or similar vessel (the handle was reunited with the other parts by John Shepherd).

miscellaneous

G100 [10] <83> OA11 (Fig 33)
Incomplete, pinched trail in curve: d *c* 50mm; scar internally from being broken off.

G101 [10] <91> OA11
Several walling fragments, presumably from bottles/beakers.

G102 [10] <131> OA11 (Fig 31)
Wall fragment: d *c* 70mm, moulded with lozenge reticulation. Probably from a beaker.

G103 [11] <129> B12 (Fig 31)
End fragment of pinched trail: surviving l 14mm, w 16mm.

G104 [500] <263> B14 (Fig 31)
Walling fragment with four horizontal trails.

G105 [500] <264> B14 (Fig 31)
Triangular-section strip, ground to shape on broadest side: surviving l 33mm, 6mm x 2mm. Presumably intended to be a decorative mount on a mirror etc.

G106 [500] <277> B14
Fragment with trails.

G107 [500] <278> B14
?Base.

G108 [500] <303> B14
Various small fragments.

Blue

beaker

G109 [10] <3> OA11 (Fig 33)
Two wall fragments: d 80mm, with moulded horizontal ribbing and white trail at rim.

plate

G110 [10] <40> OA11 (Fig 31)
Fragment from edge of well: d at surviving edge approx 200mm.

vessels of uncertain form

G111 [10] <8> OA11 (Fig 33)
Flaring base: d 80mm (not perfectly circular), with hollow stem. Possibly from a cup.

G112 [10] <9> OA11 (Fig 33)
Fragment of vertical rim of vessel moulded with spiralled ridges ?alternating with rows of droplets: d c 40mm.

G113 [10] <10> OA11
Fragment of bevelled, neatly folded rim of thin glass: d 85mm; slightly distorted; wt 1.7g.

?From a bowl etc (this unfamiliar form may not have received its final shaping).

G114 [10] <11> OA11 (Fig 34)
Plain, folded rim (forming flat lip w 4mm): d 80mm.
?From a drinking vessel – the form is unfamiliar.

G115 [10] <94> OA11
Two small walling fragments, one plain, one with moulded chequer.
Possibly from a beaker (or beakers), possibly chequered-spiral decoration.

G116 [10] <117> OA11 (Fig 31)
Fragment folded at vertical rim: d c 140mm.
Possibly a jar (John Shepherd).

Pale green

bottles

BASES (ALL ARE PUSHED-IN)
G117 [10] <7, 28–31, 65–73> OA11
D between c 50mm and c 100mm.

G118 [10] <73> OA11 (Fig 31)
D c 25mm.

G119 [10] <324> OA11
Two fragments: d c 45mm+.

G120 [93] <133> B3
D 60mm+.

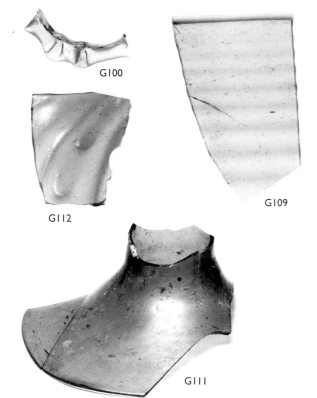

G100

G112

G109

G111

Fig 33 Post-medieval glass 5

RIMS (ALL ARE PLAIN, HORIZONTAL)
G121 [10] <20–3, 25, 85> OA11 (Fig 31)
D c 30–35mm.
G122 [75] <135> OA11
D 32mm.

PLAIN WALLING FRAGMENTS
G123 [10] <326> OA11
Several, various thicknesses and diameters.

G124 [10] <–> OA11
Three (one decayed).

G125 [44] <258> OA11

G126 [500] <275> B14
Tiny fragment.

Plate glass

Colourless

The fragments listed here seem to correspond with the factory's known output from c 1691 to the end of production, not before 1720, of plate glass. These pieces of crown and perhaps cylinder glass are very smooth on one face and slightly uneven from resting on a surface on the other. Waste edges comprise 85g.

G127 [44] <313> OA11
Fragments 8mm thick.

G128 [76] <312> OA11
Angled ?edge of (flat) sheet 9mm thick; wt 8g.

G129 [248] <186> OA11
Two fragments of sheet 5mm thick, one curved along one side.

G130 [321] <187> OA14 (Fig 34)
Fragment of sheet 5mm thick; grozed along one side; engraved with '*n°2 out (g) ...*' (italic script; John Shepherd suggests as an alternative reading *91/2°* ... *ie* nine and a half degrees ...) over three not quite parallel lines, and possible further, incomplete lettering below.

G131 [321] <221> OA14
Sheet 6mm thick.

G132 [500] <320> B14
Sheet 6mm thick.

G133 [509] <240> B14
Sheet 7mm thick.

G142

G130

G134

G114

G138

G166

Fig 34 Post-medieval glass 6

G134 [unstratified] <101> (Fig 34)
Edge of sheet 7mm thick; wt 63g.

G135 [unstratified] <111>
Sheet fragments between 4mm and 8mm thick (some slightly curved).

G136 [unstratified] <310>
Fragment with bevels along straight edge: 7mm thick; wt 14g.

Other window fragments

Colourless

G137 [10] <-> OA11
Several fragments.

G138 [248] <253> OA11 (Fig 34)
Two joining fragments with near parallel engraved pair and single lines (the former stop short of the edge).

Green

G139 [10] <60> OA11
Crown-edge fragment; wt 3.4g.

G140 [10] <323> OA11
Several crown-edge fragments; wt 19g.

G141 [248] <252> OA11
Bluish-green fragment grozed along one edge.

G142 [248] <254> OA11 (Fig 34)
Several bluish-green crown-edge fragments; wt 56g.

G143 [248] <256> OA11
Bluish-green.

G144 [248] <318> OA11
Bluish-green fragment with part of crown bullseye; wt 25g.

G145 [500] <245> B14
Bluish-green crown-edge fragment; wt 14g.

G146 [500] <248> B14 (Fig 31)
Bluish-green fragment with flanges on both faces along slightly curving edge; wt 8.9g.

G147 [500] <276> B14
Crown-edge fragment; wt 0.3g.

G148 [500] <301> B14
Variety of small fragments picked from sample.

G149 [500] <319> B14
Two fragments.

G150 [unstratified] <120>
Bluish-green crown-edge fragment; wt 3.8g.

Miscellaneous

Decayed

The following minor pieces are probably from residual glass that was unrelated to the industry.

G151 [500] <278> B14
Tiny fragment: ?window.

G152 [500] <302> B14
Small vessel fragments.

Glassworking crucibles

These distinctive, massive, vertical-walled industrial vessels were extremely robust – each would have weighed several kg even without their heavy glass contents. The fabric is coarse, dark purplish-grey or off-white. The walls are in some instances almost 50mm thick and (?with use) have a whitish, vitrified coating on both faces, which often have a further layer of vitreous dark green internally and dark brown externally; occasionally glass adheres sufficiently thickly to allow its true colour to be established (only green in those listed). Comprises >30kg.

G153 [7] <106> OA11
4.155kg of fragments.

G154 [10] <108> OA11
Fragments with greyish slag and brown glassy coatings; wt 6.54kg.

G155 [76] <97> OA11
Four shoeboxes of fragments; total wt 18.15kg – includes some with pale green glass up to 30mm thick and surviving to h 175mm.

G156 [329] <196> OA11
Sliver of rim of purplish-grey fabric; dark green glass adhering; wt 19g.

G157 [347] <195> OA7
Rim fragment of off-white fabric; thin coating of glass is streaked brown and red towards top on both sides; wt 730g.

G158 [500] <198> B14
Several walling fragments, purplish-grey fabric; some with glass adhering (dark green internally, dark brown externally – may have come off some pieces): d c 650mm; wt 3.31kg.

G159 [500] <300> B14
Several walling fragments; wt 1.25kg.

G160 [507] <197> OA11
Walling fragment of dark grey fabric; streaked dark green glass externally only; wt 258g.

G161 [unstratified] <109>
Fragments; wt 2.37kg.

G162 [unstratified] <271> (Fig 31)
Squared corner of vessel h c 75mm;

wt 155g; traces of green/opaque white glass internally, and dark brown coating externally.

G163 [unstratified] <272>
Walling fragment with vertical grooves; wt 520g; dark green glass internally and over breaks, and dark brown coating externally.

?Furnace fabric

G166–7 could be lids, or slabs used as working surfaces, etc. Comprises over 12kg.

G164 [7] <143> OA11
Fragment of coarse, pale yellowish fabric (partly obscured by ?rust), th c 37mm, with dark-coloured (?purplish) glass apparently mixed in on one side and forming a coating with an unevenly broken surface there; wt 153g.

G165 [43] <105> OA11
Substantial fragments of heat-altered, fairly coarse sandstone, possibly hassock (identified by Ian Betts), with single or adjacent two surfaces coated with dark green or dark brown glassy deposit; wt 11.155kg.

G166 [500] <199> B14 (Fig 34)
Two fragments of coarse, pale buff fabric, th c 33mm, with dark brown, glassy coating on one face, the larger fragment thickening to c 45mm at part of a ?round hole (??d c 30mm) through the fabric; combined wt 675g.
    Possibly a part of the structure with a monitoring hole, or a ?cover.

G167 [507] <200> B14
Two flat, two-layered fragments, fired dark on

both faces, th up to 26mm; one with one straight edge, the other with a dark brown glassy coating on one face; combined wt 166g. (See also G20.)

Coal

[500] <299> B14
c 500g of larger (up to 30mm) pieces hand picked from original sample of mixed material.

Possible industrial moulds

The powdery fabric of these fragments is unusual. The very smooth surface on one face means they could be from moulds (though the form of any products are difficult to define); alternatively, the flat ones could be props/supports or covers, while the concave/convex pieces might perhaps be from unfired crucibles. The first three items came from a deposit which also produced glassworking waste.

[329] <193> OA11
Fragments with flat smooth surfaces.

[329] <237> OA11
Two fragments, one with a slightly concave smooth surface, the other with a slightly convex one.

[329] <238> OA11
Fragment with join of two nearly flat, smooth surfaces.

[402] <194> OA16
Fragments with flat, smooth surfaces.

4

The animal bones

Jane Liddle

The animal bone recovered from the Benbow House excavations were derived mainly from horses. A total of 108 bones (over 36kg) were from horses, in comparison with 36 cattle bones (5.7kg). Dog bones were also common, with a total of 63 bones (3.5kg) recovered, mainly from Period 4. Very little diversity was apparent in the assemblage, with only one roe deer bone and three chicken bones present in addition to horse, dog and domesticates.

Domesticates were present in small numbers throughout Periods 2 to 5. Their presence is most likely to be residual and such small amounts, mainly present in single figures, is indicative of a spread of refuse and domestic waste around the area. The lack of diversity in the species present is also indicative of a general domestic waste assemblage that could have accumulated over time and would not have necessarily originated from the immediate vicinity or the building debris/dumping layers in which they were excavated.

Butchery

Butchery was common on all species present, including dog and horse. Its presence was defined by the cuts on the bones indicating the techniques of food preparation used as well as skinning and slaughter methods. It is noteworthy that an absence of butchery evidence does not necessarily indicate the absence of butchery. Each butchery mark visible is in effect a mistake, the ideal situation being the disarticulated or defleshed bone showing no knife marks. Each mark indicates a slip of the knife into the bone and results in the undesirable outcome of the knife being blunted.

Horse

All of the 58 butchered horse remains were recovered from Period 4 contexts. A poleaxe wound on a skull was indicative of slaughter techniques. Skinning marks were present on 17 individual bones, mainly metapodials and feet. Preliminary splitting of the carcass was evident on four bones including two mandibles. Disarticulation of the carcass was evident on 14 bones, which were dominated by upper fore limbs with one skull showing evidence of decapitation. Nine horse bones were cut during jointing, five of which also showed evidence of marrow extraction. Defleshing was also a common form of butchery, evident on a total of 17 bones. This method was most prevalent on femora and radii, with three mandibles also having evidence of cheek meat removal. The presence of most body parts, including heads and feet, indicates that the horses were being brought into the site in their entirety, straight from the knacker's yard.

Butchery on the horse bones indicates a number of uses of the carcass. Skinning was carried out followed by disarticulation and meat removal. The gnawing evidence on horse bones was not extensive and could suggest that the meat was being removed from the bones for consumption by the dogs being used in baiting and recorded as living in the kennels adjacent. Markham writing in 1633 actually recommended that 'hunting hounds' be fed 'horse-flesh newly slain, and warm at the feeding' (Markham 1633, 17). During the Tudor period, as today, horse meat was not commonly part of the human diet. No evidence of horses being eaten during the medieval period has been recorded at all within London (Rackham 1995a, 20).

Dog

Approximately a fifth of the dog bones from Benbow House showed evidence of butchery, all of which were adult and derived from Period 4. Skinning was noted on a skull and two tibiae, and defleshing on a total of six long bones. The presence of these forms of butchery is indicative of the dogs being first skinned, then defleshed, with the meat probably being fed back to the dogs. Harcourt described that the best way to skin and deflesh a dog was to hang it by its hind legs, skin it, then quickly remove the meat (Harcourt 1974, 171).

Size

Measurements to determine withers heights were available from 18 dog long bones and 18 horse bones, all from Period 4 (Table 5).

Horse

Horse sizes gave a range of size in hands between 13.2 and 16.3 hands high (1325–1652mm). An average height of 15 hands was calculated (1475mm) from these figures. This averages at the approximate size of a Welsh cob (Rackham 1995b) and is well within the typical size range of the Tudor period in London, including the large quantity of horses found at Elverton Street (Pipe & Cowie 1998). The sizes vary from draught pony to riding horse.

Dog

The dogs had an average withers height of 719mm. This average was calculated from a range of 130mm of which three bones were around 640–650mm and the remainder between 720–770mm in height, indicating that at least two sizes of

Table 5 *Withers heights from animal bones in Period 4, using von den Driesch and Boessneck (1974) and Harcourt (1974)*

species	range (mm)	mean (mm)	no.
Dog	637–768	719	18
Horse	1325–1652	1475	18

dog were represented. Three dog skulls were excavated from Open Area 13, one was whole (skull 1), one only had the muzzle remaining (skull 2) and the other was only the cranium and occipital area. A selection of measurements could be taken from the complete and near complete skulls (Table 6). The third skull, although unmeasurable, was of a similar size to the others and was from a similarly sized individual.

The dog skulls and long bones indicate that the dogs were of a considerable size. The three smaller long bones belonged to animals approximately the size of the reference Alsatian (Museum of London Specialist Services reference collection) with a shoulder height of 600mm, and the larger bones would have been from dogs at least 100–180mm taller in height. The skulls were larger in length than the reference Alsatian, although the general muzzle shape was similar. In comparison with the skulls from Vinegar Yard (Rielly in prep) the Benbow House dogs had a similar size muzzle, but with a longer cranium and narrower palate. Rielly described the dogs from Vinegar Yard as being comparable in size to mastiffs.

Stow writing in 1598 mentioned the use of mastiffs at the Bear Gardens. These, he commented, were kept in adjoining kennels. It can therefore be suggested through the size of the dogs, and documentary evidence, that they were mastiffs and were being used at the animal-baiting areas at Bankside.

Age

The two main age estimation methods employed are based on tooth eruption/wear, after Grant (1975; 1982), for cattle, sheep/goat and pigs, and epiphyseal fusion, following the age sequence shown in Schmid (1972), for all domesticates including horse and dog. All tooth wear was calculated using mandibular teeth.

Ages were not available for all bones. Mature bones are more solid than young bones and therefore preservation is on the whole better with the chance of damage caused by gnawing, and erosion in the ground, being reduced.

Table 6 *Size of dog skulls from Benbow House, including comparison with Vinegar Yard, Southwark (Rielly in prep)*

		GL (mm)	SI (mm)	SWI (mm)	PI (mm)
Benbow House	skull (1)	253.5	49.5	41.0	67.9
	skull (2)	–	–	39.5	68.9
Vinegar Yard	skull (1)	218.2	49.8	41.8	70.8
	skull (2)	235.0	49.4	42.0	76.2

GL is the greatest length. Snout Index (SI) and Snout Width Index (SWI) taken from Harcourt (1974, 153–4). Palate Index (PI) equals width at the first molars x 100/palate length (P-St) (von den Driesch 1976).

Small bones and small mammal bones are usually retrieved during wet-sieving and due to the absence of much bone being collected in this way, small and young bones will also be missing from the assemblage. Nevertheless the comparison of those bones available with fusion data and the addition of mandible wear patterns give an indication of the approximate ages available from the site. In addition the presence of neonate and infant bones has been recorded, thus giving an estimate of numbers present, even without specific fusion data.

Horse

In total 69 horse bones had epiphyseal fusion data, and four mandibles showed wear patterns. One was from Period 5, the remainder from Period 4.

It is evident that all horse bones with epiphyseal data were from mature animals, shown by the largest amount of epiphyseal information being gained from late fusing bones. In light of the large number of whole horse bones, this is indicative of most horses at the site being adult and at least 3.5 years of age. One metapodial was unfused at the distal end,

indicating it was under a year old. This individual may have been a sickly or injured animal that was slaughtered prior to maturity. Mandibular wear data also indicated that mature animals were most common.

Dog

Ageing data for dogs derive only from epiphyseal fusion. All but one of a total of 30 bones with epiphyseal fusion were fused. One late fusing bone came from Period 5, all of the rest from Period 4; most were from an external dump, context [700].

A single unfused tibia from Period 4 is the only evidence of a young dog at the site. This individual would have been under a year and a half old, therefore if it were a baiting dog that died at this age it may have been an unlucky victim of the sport with which it was associated. The remainder of the dogs would have been at least a year and a half old.

It should be noted that age, size and stature, and ageing analysis was also carried out for domesticates other than horse and dog but is not included in this report.

5

The clay tobacco pipes

Kieron Heard

The excavations produced 261 fragments of clay tobacco pipe, of which 140 are bowls. Apart from four probable Broseley types, it is likely that all of the pipes were made locally. There is no evidence, such as wasters, kiln debris or structures, to indicate pipe manufacture on the site. A relatively large proportion (*c* 37%) of the pipe bowls bear makers' marks, but unfortunately few of these can be attributed. There are seven decorated pipes. The pipes are mostly of mid 17th- to late 18th-century date, with a few dating to the 19th century.

Most of the pipe bowls have been classified according to the Chronology of Bowl Types (Atkinson & Oswald 1969). The Simplified General Typology (Oswald 1975) has been used to obtain closer dating for some of the 18th-century pipes. The prefixes AO and OS are used here to indicate which typology has been applied.

Marked pipes

Moulded initials on either side of the heel or spur

AA AO21 1680–1710 Two examples, from different moulds. The initials read at right angles to the line of the stem, rather than parallel which was the convention [unstratified] <280> <281>
AA AO22 1680–1710 The maker's initials are oriented as above [unstratified] <126>
AA AO25 1700–70 Three examples, from two different moulds [44] <156>; [54/55] <52>, [74] <154>
AA OS10 1700–40 Four examples, from two different moulds [unstratified] <125> <282>; [500] <204> [507] <293>

There are 10 examples of pipes of the late 17th and early 18th centuries bearing the initials AA. Pipes with this mark occur most frequently in this part of London and are usually attributed to the maker Anthony (Arthur) Andrews who is recorded as working in Southwark during the period 1694–1716 (Oswald 1975, 130).

IA AO25 1700–70 [74] <148>
IA OS11 1730–60 [248] <206>

NA/SH AO27? 1780–1820 A large bowl with thin walls and an unusual combination of moulded double initials, possibly

indicating a pipemaking partnership. Two examples from the same mould [407] <171> <172>

IB AO25 1700–70 [unstratified] <283>
IB OS11 1730–60 Five examples, probably from different moulds [248] <284> <285> <286> <287> <288>
IB AO27 1780–1820 Large bowl with thin walls. Two examples from the same mould [407] <170> <289>

TB AO25 1700–70 [unstratified] <122>
TB AO27 1780–1820 Large bowl with thin walls [407] <168>

TC AO27 1780–1820 Large bowl with thin walls [407] <169>

IH Heel only, but probably dated 1680–1710 [507] <295>

JH AO29 1840–80 Ridged seams with 'ears of wheat' decoration [309] <179>

IM AO27 1780–1820 Large bowl with thin walls. Two examples from the same mould [407] <173> <290>

HS OS12 1730–80 [unstratified] <53>

WS AO25 1700–70 Five examples, from three or four different moulds. Small initials [unstratified] <124>; [75] <146>. Large

initials [74] <153>. Large initials with S recut [74] <147> <152>

TW AO25 1700–70 Four examples from the same mould [74] <149> <150> <151> <155>
TW AO27 1780–1820 Two examples from different moulds. Large bowls [330] <175> <176>
TW AO28 1820–40 Large bowl decorated with Masonic symbols, and with a flower and leaf motif on the front seam [330] <174> (Fig 35)

A? Heel only, but probably dated 1680–1710 [507] <294>

W? AO25 1700–70 [75] <145>

?? OS10 1700–40 [unstratified] <203>
?? AO28 1820–40 Decorated with a large bunch of grapes on either side of the bowl [321] <201>

Moulded symbols on either side of the heel or spur

Asterisk AO28 1820–40 Reeded bowl. Also marked along the stem in a panel surrounded by a floral motif: T. WOOT ... / ... ST. BORO [336] <180> (Fig 35)

The maker was Thomas Wootten, who is recorded as working in nearby Park Street,

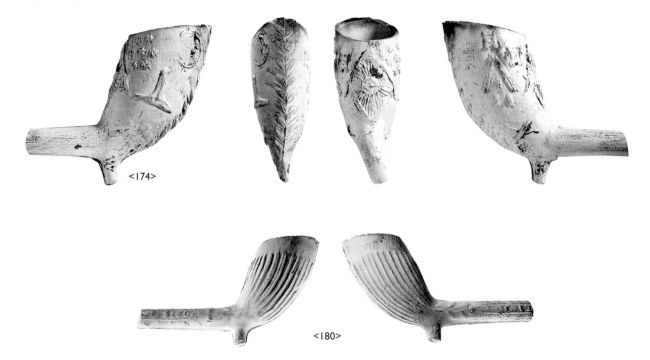

Fig 35 Two clay tobacco pipes by Thomas Wootten of Park Street, Borough 1820–46: large bowl decorated with Masonic symbols, and flower and leaf motif on seam <174> and reeded bowl marked along the stem in a panel T. WOOT ... / ... ST. BORO <180>

Borough during the period 1820–46 (Oswald 1975, 149). Other 19th-century pipes with the moulded initials TW (see above) can probably be attributed to him.

Crowns OS10 1700–40 Two examples, from different moulds [500] <291> <292>

Pierced star AO27 1780–1820 'Ears of wheat' seam decoration [302] <206>

Decorated pipes

Apart from the examples described above, there are two other decorated pipes.

A type AO26 bowl (1740–1800) decorated with the Royal Arms of the House of Hanover. On the back of the bowl are a large rose and thistle, either side of the white horse of Hanover surmounted by an escutcheon charged with the crown of Charlemagne. Below is a ribbon carrying the motto DIEU ET MON DROIT, and above is a large crown. On either side of the bowl are the initials GR, referring possibly to George II (1727–60) or George III (1760–1820). On the front of the bowl is a church spire

with a cockerel perched on top. This design has been recorded previously, from the Thames foreshore at Paul's Wharf (Le Cheminant 1981, 125, no. 32). [unstratified] <51>

A fragment from a type AO26 bowl (1740–1800), the complete design of which is known from an example published previously (Le Cheminant 1981, 126, no. 35). Ninepins are moulded on the left side of the bowl and on the right a bewigged man in a loose shirt and breeches is about to bowl a cheese at them. On the front of the bowl is a large tree in full leaf. In the background is what looks like a fisherman on a pier. A very similar pipe from the kiln of William Heath in Brentford bears the initials HB and is attributed by Le Cheminant to the maker Henry Blundell, working in Unicorn Alley, Borough 1745–64. [unstratified] <123>

Broseley pipes

There are four bowls which are probably from Broseley, Shropshire. They can be compared with examples illustrated by Oswald (1975, 51). It is very unusual for

regional bowl types to be found in the London area. All the examples here are unstratified.

Large, forward-leaning, bulbous bowl with thick walls and a heart-shaped base. The bowl rim is almost fully milled. The stem is thick. Similar to Oswald's type 5a (1680–1730) [unstratified] <61>

Similar to the above, but with a splayed heel and a thinner stem. Similar to Oswald's type 5a (1680–1730) [unstratified] <62>

Large, barrel-shaped bowl with thick walls and a heart-shaped base. Half of the bowl rim is milled. Similar to Oswald's type 1c (1670–80) [unstratified] <63>

Large, forward-leaning, bulbous bowl with a very pronounced heart-shaped base. There is an incised line around half of the bowl rim. The stem is thick. Similar to Oswald's type 5a (1680–1730) [unstratified] <64>

All of the above have fired to a greyish white colour. Generally they are poorly finished, with irregular milling around the rim and mould lines which have not been erased completely.

6

Conclusions

The archaeological works at Benbow House, although limited in scope by the strategy of preservation *in situ* of archaeological deposits not under threat of destruction, have produced a wealth of new information on Bankside in the medieval and post-medieval periods.

The site, located beside the Thames, was in an area of land that was not inhabited until the medieval period due to its marginal location. The deposit of peat dated to the Bronze Age and frequently found in north Southwark is evidence of a period of regression allowing the build-up of marshland vegetation.

The earliest extant evidence of human activity recorded on the site was associated with an attempt at consolidation in the 12th or 13th century. The land was owned by the bishop of Winchester and was embanked from the early 14th century. Although no direct evidence of embanking was found, it is probable that the development of embankments was associated with the deposition of a thick deposit of crushed chalk. This was sufficient to stabilise the ground, without the need for timber piling, for construction of a number of chalk-walled buildings. The buildings are dated to the 14th and 15th centuries and are interpreted as the remains of 'stews' – inns or brothels known from documentary sources to line this part of Bankside in the medieval period. It is likely some of the individual buildings recorded at Benbow House are the stews known as The Bell & Cock and The Unicorn. One building (B7) had a cellar and a garderobe or drain that either emptied into or was flushed by the river. Unfortunately no full ground plan was recovered for any of these buildings. There was also evidence of deep cut features set back from the river, and these are thought to be fish ponds, some of which are shown on early maps of the area. One of these features contained a large dump of Surrey Whiteware similar to material recovered from excavations at Eden Street, Kingston (Miller & Stephenson 1999).

In the 16th and 17th centuries Bankside was known for its entertainments, and was at one time the location of two animal-baiting arenas (see Figs 11 and 12). Building 2, recorded during the evaluation phase of the investigations, may have been associated with animal-baiting and was preserved *in situ* rather than the subject of full excavation. Building 12 may be the post-1583 rebuild of an arena following its documented collapse. A postulated plan of the structure indicates that it was multi-sided (with up to 12 sides) and had an internal diameter of *c* 16.0m. A large deposit of horse and dog bones was found nearby. Analysis of butchery marks on the bones has led to the conclusion that old, mature horses may have been fed to dogs that were kept for use in the arena.

Bears were involved in animal-baiting and perhaps the most surprising evidence from the site is the total lack of bear bones. The list of livestock involved in the transaction of buying the lease for Bear Gardens in 1590 was quite substantial, including nine bears, three bulls, a horse and an ape (Kingsford 1920, 174–5). The bears would have been prized possessions, some being bought in the lease for up to £10. Presumably they were unlikely to die during baiting or if they did the carcass would have been taken elsewhere – possibly fetching a reasonable price for the pelt.

Contemporary documents also indicate that bulls were being baited at Bear Gardens, such as the description by Paul Hentzner, a German visiting in 1598 (Bowers 1902), who mentioned a 'theatre, for the baiting of bulls and bears'. Cattle bones excavated from Benbow House were dispersed and no obvious dumping was apparent.

Physical evidence from the dog bones indicates that they were of mastiff size and stature. This fits well with the many references to mastiffs being used for baiting. Three smaller dogs recovered were still large and would have been of an adequate size for baiting and may have been just another breed of an English bulldog. The dogs were mature, with few incidences of pathology. An ossified haematoma on a tibia was possibly the result of a blunt impact (Baker & Brothwell cited in Ainsley 1998). This may have resulted from a wound sustained during fighting. Once the dogs had died, or been killed, butchery evidence indicates that they were being skinned and filleted. The skins would have been used for fabric and the meat may possibly have been fed back to the rest of the dogs.

Building 12 is not thought to be the Hope theatre, which was built in 1613 to replace the old bearbaiting arena. Documentary and recent archaeological work (Blatherwick 1998; Cowan 1999) indicate the Hope was either further south or, more likely, further to the east.

The presence of pottery forms such as money boxes, drinking jugs and the Raeren panel jug (see Fig 17) are a further reflection of the entertainment or recreational nature of Bankside.

Medieval building B7 was reused and infilled with a large amount of tin-glazed pottery (delftware), providing evidence of the later industrial function of Bankside. The Bear Gardens pothouse was in operation from 1702 to no later than 1710 but was not the first pottery on the site, another existing before 1671. A glasshouse was also present from at least 1671 and had possibly ceased production by 1748. Deposits from the site contain important evidence of the products of the glasshouse.

From at least 1748 to the late 19th century there was a foundry on Bankside. From 1780 this was run by the Bradley family, with James Benbow becoming sole owner in the period 1835–8. A furnace was found, and brick buildings, unfortunately not fully excavated, are thought to have had ancillary functions. Certainly Building 26 appears from its recovered ground plan to have been a specialised building with numerous small rooms or bays. A foundry was still in operation on Bankside in 1895; metalworking debris recovered included numerous examples of iron and copper-alloy buckles being produced here. Other buildings recorded at Benbow House included a domestic building (B20) overlooking the Thames and with fireplaces in four of the rooms.

7

French and German summaries

Résumé

Ce rapport présente les résultats de travaux de fouille et d'évaluation à Benbow House, Bankside dans l'arrondissement de Southwark entre 1995 et 1999 (TQ 3223 8051) (Museum of London code de site BAN95).

Le site se situe près de la Tamise, mais à une certaine distance du quartier de l'avenue principale de l'arrondissement, qui avait été le centre principal d'activité à l'époque médiévale et romaine. Une couche de terre tourbeuse datant de l'Âge du Bronze, ainsi que d'autres couches de sols en bord d'eau, montrent que le terrain a été soumis à la montée et la baisse des eaux de la Tamise pendant une longue période (OA1).

L'évidence importante et la plus ancienne d'activité humaine dans la zone de fouille fut une tentative de consolidation de terrain pendant le XIIème ou XIIIème siècle (OA2). Cette activité externe fut suivie par trois périodes de construction datant du XIIIème siècle et après. Une couche épaisse de craie écrasée couvrant toute la zone de fouille avait été employée pour stabiliser le sol antérieurement à la construction des bâtiments (OA3). En tout, neuf ou dix bâtiments ont pu être datés aux XIIIème et XIVème siècles (B1–B10). Les bâtiments avaient des murs de craie et comprenaient probablement les restes des "stews" – auberges ou maisons de prostitution identifiés d'après des sources documentaires comme étant "The Bell & Cock" et "The Unicorn". Un dépotoire de céramique de type "Surrey Whiteware" fut retrouvé dans une fosse à l'exterieur et au sud des Bâtiments 5 et 9 (OA9).

D'autres bâtiments furent bâtis sur le site aux XVIème et XVIIème siècles dont possiblement une deuxième phase au Bâtiment 2. À l'ouest un autre bâtiment a été interprété comme étant peut-être un chenil (B11). Une activité externe dans le coin sud-est du site (OA12) fut suivie par la construction de ce qui semblerait être un grand bâtiment à plusieurs côtés (B12), peut-être était-ce l'arène de combats d'animaux connue grâce à l'évidence cartographique et documentaire. Une large quantité d'os de cheval et de chien furent retrouvé dans des couches associées avec le Bâtiment 12 (OA13). L'évidence de la boucherie de chevaux essentiellement vieux peut suggérer que ces animaux servaient à l'alimentation des chiens gardés à côté pour les combats d'animaux et de chiens. Au nord du Bâtiment 12, un dépotoir de poterie glaçée à l'étain (dite "delftware"), trouvé dans une cave médiévale réutilisée (B13), fournit la première évidence archéologique de la fabrique de poterie sur le site des "Bear Gardens" (ce qui signifie "arènes de combats d'ours") qui fut en activité de 1702 à 1710. D'autres dépotoirs fouillés dans des zones externes (OA5–OA8 et OA10–OA11) comprenaient des tessons de verre et des débris importants du travail du verre, provenant probablement d'une verrerie qui commença à fonctionner en 1671 et cessa en 1748.

La dernière phase des trouvailles archéologiques inclut les vestiges de bâtiments en brique datant du XVIIIème et XIXème siècle (B14–B29) réflètant l'emploi ultérieur du site comme fonderie et travail des métaux, entreprise possédée par la Famille Bradley et ultérieurement par James Benbow.

Ces bâtiments ne furent pas complètement fouillés, et bien que les restes d'un four furent trouvés, il semblerait que celui-ci ait eu principalement une fonction auxilliaire. Les débris du travail des métaux incluaient de nombreux exemples de boucles. Entre les bâtiments B20 et B25 (OA14) se situaient des zones externes et d'autres fouilles furent faites à l'est des bâtiments B14–16 (OA15). Celles-ci révélèrent l'évidence d'égouts industriels.

La fouille archéologique de "Benbow House" est un exemple de la tendance récente vers une préservation des restes archéologiques *in situ*, avec la fouille limitée seulement aux zones où les couches archéologiques seront totalement et inévitablement détruites durant le chantier de construction. Ce choix de démarche archéologique à "Benbow House" aboutit seulement à une enquête partielle de l'arène présumée et des bâtiments en brique du XVIIIème et XIXème siècle. Ces structures ont été conservées où elles étaient présentes en dessous de 3,70m NG, le niveau le plus bas de destruction causée par la dalle en béton du nouveau bâtiment. Ailleurs sur le site, le nouveau sous-sol du parking et les positions des pilliers en béton entraînèrent la fouille de toutes les couches archéologiques, et ce fut là que l'on concentra le travail archéologique.

Zusammenfassung

In diesem Bericht werden die Ergebnisse der Test- und endgültigen Ausgrabungsarbeiten während der Jahre 1995-99 im Benbow House, Bankside, Southwark, dargelegt (TQ 3223 8051) (MoL Grabungskode BAN95).

Die Grabungsstätte liegt direkt an der Themse, jedoch ein Stück von dem Borough Highstreet-Gebiet entfernt, wo sich die Aktivitäten in römischer und mittelalterlicher Zeit konzentrierten. Eine auf die Bronzezeit datierte Torflage und andere den Fluten ausgesetzte Lagen zeigen, daß das Land für lange Zeit den wechselnden Wasserständen der Themse ausgesetzt war (OA1).

Der früheste Hinweis auf menschliche Tätigkeit im Grabungsgebiet, ein Versuch das Land zu befestigen, ist für das 12. oder 13. Jahrhundert belegt (OA2). Vom 13. Jahrhundert an folgten diesen Außenarbeiten drei Bauperioden. Eine dicke, sich über die gesamte Fläche erstreckende, grobkörnige Kreideschicht stabilisierte den Untergrund für die Errichtung von Gebäuden (OA3). Insgesamt können neun oder zehn Gebäude ins 13. und 14. Jahrhundert datiert werden (B1-B10). Die Gebäude standen auf Kreidefundamenten und sind wahrscheinlich die Reste von 'stews', d. h. Wirtshäusern oder Bordellen, für die dokumentarische Quellen vorhanden sind,

wie z. B. die Pubs 'Bell and Cock' und 'Unicorn'. Außerhalb der nach Süden gelegenen Gebäude B5 und B9 (in OA9) lagen in einer Grube Surrey-White-Ware Scherben.

Weitere Gebäudereste aus dem 16. und 17. Jahrhundert mögen eine zweite Phase des Gebäudes B2 darstellen. Westlich davon könnte ein anderes Gebäude, ein Hundezwinger, gestanden haben (B11). Externen Aktivitäten in der Südostecke (OA12) folgte, wie es scheint, der Bau eines großen mehreckigen Gebäudes (B12), möglicherweise einer Tierhatz-Arena, für die dokumentarische und kartographische Unterlagen existieren. Von auswärtigen Lagen (OA13), die mit dem Gebäude B12 in Zusammenhang stehen, stammen eine große Anzahl Pferde- und Hundeknochen. Anzeichen für das Schlachten vorwiegend alter Pferde mögen darauf hinweisen, daß sie an Hunde verfüttert wurden, die in der Nachbarschaft für die Tierhatz gehalten wurden. Nördlich vom Gebäude B12 wurde in einem wiederbenutzten, mittelalterlichen Keller (B13) ein Abfallhaufen mit zinnglasierter Töpfer- (oder Delftware) freigelegt, der den ersten ausgegrabenen Beweis für das Vorhandensein der Bear Garden Töpferei liefert, die dort von 1702 bis1710 in Betrieb war. Andere Abfallhaufen, die außerhalb der Gebäude lagen (OA5-OA8 und OA10-OA11), enthielten wichtige Glas- und bearbeitete Glasreste, die wahrscheinlich von einer nahegelegenen Glasbläserei stammen, die 1671 den Betrieb aufnahm und ihn um 1748 wieder eingestellt hatte.

Die letzte Phase enthielt Ziegelgebäude aus dem 18. und 19. Jahrhundert (B14-B29), die auf die Nutzung der Fläche für Gießerei und Metallverarbeitung deuten, sie gehörten erst der Bradley Familie und später James Benbow. Obwohl die Überreste eines Schmelzofens gefunden wurden, wurden diese Gebäude nicht vollständig ausgegraben, da sie wohl hauptsächlich nur untergeordneten Aufgaben dienten. Zu den Überresten der Metallbearbeitung gehörten zahlreiche Schnallen. Die externen Gebiete zwischen den Gebäuden B20 und B25 (OA14) und östlich der Gebäude B14-B16 (OA15) wurden teilweise ausgegraben und enthielten industrielle Drainagen.

Die Benbow House Arbeiten sind ein Beispiel für den neuerlichen Trend der Bewahrung archäologischer Reste in situ, während vollständige Ausgrabungen nur in solchen Gegenden vorgenommen werden, wo die archäologischen Lagen unvermeidbar und vollständig durch Neubautätigkeit zerstört würden. Die Akzeptanz dieses Trends bedeutet, daß die vermutete Hatz-Arena und die Gebäude aus dem 18. und 19. Jahrhundert nur teilweise untersucht werden konnten. Die Gebäudereste bleiben erhalten, wo sie gegenwärtig unterhalb 3,70m OD liegen, dem niedrigsten Zerstörungsniveau, das von den Neubauten erreicht werden kann. Anderenorts zwang der Bau eines neuen Parkhauses auf Pfeilern, alle Kulturlagen auszugraben, sodaß die archäologischen Arbeiten sich auf dieses Gebiet konzentrierten.

APPENDIX: POTTERY EXPANSION CODES

Fabric codes

Fabric	Expansion	Range
Medieval		
CBW	Coarse Border wares (rare pre-1300, common c 1350)	1270–1500
CBW BIF	Cooking pots with bifid rims	1380–1500
CBW FT	Cooking pots with flat-topped rims	1340–1500
CHEA	Cheam Whiteware	1350–1500
EMSH	Early Medieval Shelly ware 1050?	1050–1150
FKING	Fine Kingston-type ware	1320–1400
KING	Kingston-type ware (poss from 1200)	1230–1400
LANG	Langerwehe Stoneware	1350–1500
LARA	Langerwehe/Raeren Stoneware	1450–1500
LCOAR	Coarse London-type ware	1080–1200
LLON	Late London ware	1400–1500
LMHG	Late Medieval Hertfordshire Green-glazed ware	1340–1450
LOGR	Local Grey ware (poss from 1020)	1050–1150
LOND	London-type ware	1080–1350
MG	Mill Green ware	1270–1350
SAIG	Smooth Green-glazed Saintonge ware	1280–1350
SAIM	Mottled Green-glazed Saintonge ware	1250–1650
SHER	South Herts/Limpsfield Greywares	1140–1300
SIEG	Siegburg Unglazed Stoneware	1300–1500
SSW	Shelly Sandy ware (1100+?)	1140–1220
TUDG	Tudor Green ware	1350–1500
Post-medieval		
BEAY	Beauvais Yellow-glazed ware	1500–1600
BISC	Biscuit-fired Delftware	1570–1800
BORD	Border ware	1550–1700
BORDG	Green-glazed Border ware	1550–1700
BORDY	Yellow-glazed Border ware	1550–1700
CHPO	Chinese Porcelain (rare before 1650)	1580–1900
CHPO ROSE	Famille Rose	1720–1800
CREA	Creamware	1740–1880
CSTN	Cistercian ware	1480–1600
DUTR	Dutch Red Earthenware	1300–1650
DUTSL	Dutch Slip-coated ware	1500–1650
EBORD	Early Border ware	1480–1550

Fabric	Expansion	Range
ENGS	English Stoneware	1700–1900
FREC	Frechen Stoneware	1550–1700
INDV	Misc industrial vessels	1480–1900
KILNF	Kiln furniture	1480–1900
LANG	Langerwehe Stoneware	1480–1550
LONS	London Stoneware	1670–1900
MART 1	Type I (buff earthenware)	1480–1550
MART 2	Type II (dark brown stoneware)	1500–1600
MOCH	Mocha ware	1780–1900
MPUR	Midlands Purple ware	1480–1750
PEAR	Pearlware	1770–1850
PEAR BW	Blue and white painted decoration	1770–1850
PMBL	Post-medieval Black-glazed ware	1580–1700
PMR	Post-medieval Redware	1580–1900
PMRE	Early Post-medieval Redware (formerly TUDB)	1480–1600
PMSR	Post-medieval Slip-coated Redware (formerly GUYS)	1480–1650
PMSRG	Post-medieval Slip-coated Redware with green glaze (formerly GUYSG)	1480–1650
PMSRY	Post-medieval Slip-coated Redware with yellow glaze (formerly GUYSY)	1480–1650
RAER	Raeren Stoneware	1480–1610
RBOR	Red Border ware	1580–1800
RBORSL	Red Border ware with slip-trailed decoration	1580–1800
RESTG	Glazed Red Stoneware	1760–1780
SBLB	English Stoneware black-leading bottle	1800–1900
SNTG	South Netherlands Maiolica	1480–1575
SWSG	Staffs White Salt-glazed Stoneware	1720–1780
SWSG SCRB	Scratch blue decoration	1740–1780
TGW	English Tin-glazed ware	1570–1800
TGW A	Orton A (lead-glazed exterior/Wan Li/blue/yellow)	1612–1650
TGW B	Orton B (manganese glaze)	1630–1680
TGW C	Orton C (plain white glaze)	1630–1800
TGW D	Orton D (lead glaze exterior/polychrome)	1630–1680
TPW	Transfer-printed ware (underglaze)	1780–1900
TPW4	Colour transfers (green mulberry 2 colour)	1825–1900
WEST	Westerwald-type Stoneware	1590–1800

Form codes

Form	Expansion
Medieval	
BEAK	Beaker
BOWL	Bowl
CP	Cooking pot
CP FT	Flat-topped rim cooking pot
CRUC	Crucible
CUP	Cup
DISH	Dish
DJ	Drinking jug
DRIP	Dripping dish
FINI	Finial
JAKO	Jakobakanne
JUG	Jug
JUG BAL	Baluster jug
JUG PUZZ	Puzzle jug
JUG RND	Rounded jug
JUGCIST	Jug or cistern
LCUP	Lobed cup
LID	Lid
MBOX	Money box
MISC	Miscellaneous unidentified form
PIP	Pipkin
PTCH	Pitcher
-	Unidentified
Post-medieval	
ALB	Albarello
ALTVA	Altar vase
BART	Bartmann
BLACKP	Blacking paste pot
BOT	Bottle
BOWL	Bowl
BOWL HAND	Handled bowl
BOWL PNCH	Punch bowl
BUTP	Butterpot (MPUR)
CHAR	Charger
CHICK	'Chicken feeder'
CHP	Chamber pot
CNDST ORN	Ornamental candlestick
CP	Cooking pot
CRUC	Crucible

Form	Expansion
CUP	Cup
DISH	Dish
DISH FLUT	Fluted dish
DISH RECT	Rectangular dish (inc serving)
DISH SM	Small dish
DJ	Drinking jug
DRIP	Dripping dish
FLDISH	Flanged dish
FLP	Flower pot
GOB	Goblet
JAR	Jar
JAR LG	Large jar
JAR SM	Small jar
JAR ST	Storage jar
JAR STR	Straight-sided jar
JAR WD	Wet drug jar
JUG	Jug
LID	Lid
LID TPOT	Teapot lid
MBOX	Money box
MUG	Mug
OINT	Ointment pot
PIP	Pipkin
PLATE	Plate
PORR	Porringer
PORR A	TGW Shape (a) straight-sided
POSS	Posset pot
POSS CYL	Cylindrical posset pot
PTCH	Pitcher
SAGG	Saggar
SALT	Salt cellar
SAUC	Saucer
SBOAT	Sauce boat
SHELF	Shelf – kiln furniture
SKIL	Skillet
TANK	Tankard
TBOWL	Tea bowl
TCUP	Tea cup
TRIP	Tripod pitcher
WSTL	Whistle
-	Unidentified

Decoration codes

Decoration	Expansion
Medieval	
-	Unidentified
APDD	Diagonal applied strips
APRS	Applied rouletted strip
APST	Applied strip
CLGL	Clear glaze
INCW	Incised wavy or curvilinear decoration
RDS	Ring and dot stamp
RESL	Red slip
SBF	Fleur-de-lys stamped boss
STAB	Stabbed
STMP	Stamped
THBC	Continuous thumbing (basal)
THM	Thumbed
Post-medieval	
-	Unidentified
APDM	Applied relief-moulded decoration
BOSS	Bossed decoration (not stamped)
BW	Blue and white
CABL	Cable pattern (TGW)

Decoration	Expansion
CHIN	Chinese-style pattern
CREN	Crenellated
ENMD	Enamelled (overglaze painting)
FACE	Face mask (applied eg FREC LONS)
FISH	Fish decoration
FLOR	Floral decoration
FOLI	Foliate decoration
GEO	Geometric decoration
GRGL	Green glaze
INCW	Incised wavy or curvilinear decoration
INSB	Inscribed band (KOLS FREC)
INSC	Inscription
IRON	Iron-dipped rims (SWSG)
LAND	Landscape
MOLD	Moulded decoration
POLY	Polychrome
SLTR	Slip-trailed
THNK	Thumbed band round neck (PMR)
WANL	Wan Li patterns
WHSL	White slip
WILL	Willow pattern

GLOSSARY

animal-baiting The practice of baiting animals with mastiff dogs. Evidence from eyewitness accounts indicates that when bulls and bears were baited, they were chained to a stake in the centre of the baiting arena, whereas horses and ponies (sometimes with monkeys tethered to their backs) ran free within the arena. The practice of baiting bulls appears to have been connected to their slaughter for human consumption whereas the practice of baiting bears appears to have been primarily as a form of entertainment. Bears also presented the dogs with an opponent with characteristics similar to those possessed by humans and thus gave the mastiffs a quasi-human opponent. As mastiffs were also used as 'dogs of war', this provided training for the dogs and (no doubt) their human handlers.

Bank End At the eastern end of Bankside, the end of the Bank. Bank End was the location of the bishop of Winchester's tidal mills

Bankside A street parallel to the south bank of the Thames and originally linking Bank End and the manor of Paris Garden to the west. Martha Carlin (1996, 40) suggests that Bankside probably originated as a causeway or embankment. The name is now also used, more generally, to apply to a non-specific area within the vicinity of Bankside.

Bear Gardens Name of one of the north–south aligned streets running between Park Street (formerly Maid or Maiden Lane) and Bankside. Cartographic evidence, in the form of William Morgan's map ((1682), indicates that the street existed in the 1680s but, initially, did not extend as far south as Park Street.

bear gardens Term originally applied to purpose-built bearbaiting arenas but then extended to apply to associated buildings, structures etc.

bearwards Licensed by the Master of Bears and therefore able to bait bears (and presumably other animals) without falling foul of the 1572 Act for the Punishment of Vagabonds. According to Susan Cerasano (1991, 203) bearwards were 'itinerant' – presumably plying their trade outside London.

Master of the Bears A sought-after royal appointment which provided the office holder with control of the Royal Game (which was known to include lions and tigers along with bears) and of animal-baiting in both the capital and the provinces. While expected to provide entertainment to royalty and visiting dignitaries, the Master would also run baiting events, license other people to bait at the bear gardens, license bearwards and control the supply of bears and dogs. The post carried royal patronage with it plus the opportunity to make money.

Paris Garden The westernmost of the five major manors within medieval Southwark, at the southern end of modern Blackfriars Bridge.

stewholders/mongers People who ran stewhouses – *ie* brothel keepers. Of the 33 households recorded on Bankside in the Poll Tax Return of 1381, seven were stewmongers (Carlin 1996, 181).

stewhouses Properties located within the Stews and used for prostitution – *ie* brothels.

Stews/Stewside The area between Maiden Lane/Park Street and Bankside. The name appears to originate in the mid 14th century.

BIBLIOGRAPHY

Abbreviations

BAR   British Archaeological Reports
MoL   Museum of London
MoLAS   Museum of London Archaeology Service

Primary sources

Guildhall Library Maps and Manuscripts Department

MS 1513. Court Book. Manor of Southwark. 1707–41

London Metropolitan Archives

P92/SAV/1276. Plan of Shears, Bradley and Benbow's premises.
C F Maltby. Undated

Public Record Office

CP/43/776. Lease between John Stevens and others and George
Birch and John Mander. 19 November 1776

Southwark Local Studies Library

St Saviour's Poor Rate Book June 1748 to September 1766
St Saviour's Poor Rate Book February 1767 to July 1776
St Saviour's Land Tax Assessment 1775 to 1794

Maps and panoramas consulted

1544–8 *Panorama*. Wyngaerde
1572 *Londinum Feracissimi Angliae Regni Metropolis*. G Braun &
F Hogenberg
1560–90 *Civitas Londini*. Attributed to Ralph Agas
1593 *Speculum Britanniae. The first parte. An Historical and
Chorographical Description of Middlesex*. John Norden
1600 *Civitas Londini*. John Norden
1616 *Londinum Florentissima Brittanniae Urbs*. J C Visscher
c 1633 *Cittie of London*. Cornelius Dankerts (attributed to
Augustine Ryther)
1647 *Long View of London from Southwark*. Wenceslaus Hollar
1658 *An Exact Delineation of the Cities of London, Southwark
and Westminster and the Suburbs*. W Faithorne &
R Newcourt
1667 *An Exact Survey ... of the City of London*. John Leake
1682 *London Actually Survey'd and a prospect of London and
Westminster*. William Morgan
1746 *Plan of the Cities of London, Westminster and the Borough
of Southwark*. John Rocque
1792–9 *Plan of London Westminster Southwark & Parts adjoining*.
Richard Horwood
1819 *Plan of London Westminster Southwark & Parts adjoining*.
Faden edition
1863 *Ordnance Survey*. 60 inch
1875 *Ordnance Survey*. 60 inch
1893–4 *Ordnance Survey*. 60 inch
1897 *Ordnance Survey*. 1/2500
1901 *Metropolitan Borough of Southwark*. Compiled by Arthur
Harrison, Borough Engineer and Surveyor
1914 *Ordnance Survey*. 1/2500
1916 *Ordnance Survey*. 1/2500

1933 *London County Council Revision of 1919 Ordnance Survey.* 60 inch 1:1056

1946 *London County Council Revision of 1919 Ordnance Survey.* 60 inch 1:1056

1951–2 *Ordnance Survey.* 1/1250

1960 *Revision of the 1951 Ordnance Survey.* 1/1250

1970 *Ordnance Survey.* 1/1250

1995 *Ordnance Survey Superplan.* 1/1250

Catalogues, directories and dictionaries

1790 Universal British Directory of Trade and Commerce

1803 Post Office Annual Directory

1805 Post Office Annual Directory

1811 Post Office Annual Directory

1883 Post Office London Directory

1886 Post Office London Directory

1888 Post Office London Directory

1889 Post Office London Directory

1890 Post Office London Directory

1986 The Collins English Dictionary (2nd ed, 1987 reprint)

Printed sources and secondary works

Place of publication given for titles published outside the United Kingdom.

Ainsley, C, 1998 *Assessment of the animal bones from Benbow House, Bear Gardens, Bankside, SE1,* MoLAS Assessment Report

Atkinson, D R & Oswald, A, 1969 'London clay tobacco pipes', *J British Archaeol Assoc* 32, 171–227

Austin, J C, 1994 *British delft at Williamsburg,* Colonial Williamsburg Foundation, Williamsburg, VA

Baker, J & Brothwell, D, 1980 *Animal diseases in archaeology*

Blatherwick, S, 1997 'The archaeological evaluation of the Globe playhouse', in *Shakespeare's Globe rebuilt* (ed J R Mulryne & M Shewring), 66–80

Blatherwick, S, 1998 'London's pre-Restoration purpose-built theatres of the sixteenth and seventeenth centuries', English Heritage, unpub

Blatherwick, S & Densem, R, 1994 *Benbow House site, Bankside/New Globe Street, SE1: a brief documentary assessment,* MoLAS, unpub

Blatherwick, S & Gurr, A, 1992 'Shakespeare's factory: archaeological evaluations on the site of the Globe theatre', *Antiquity* 66, 251, 315–28

Boulton, J, 1987 *Neighbourhood and society: a London suburb in the seventeenth century*

Bowers, R W, 1902 *Sketches of Southwark, old and new*

Bowsher, J, 1998 *The Rose theatre: an archaeological discovery,* MoL

Bowsher, J & Blatherwick, S, 1990 'The structure of the Rose', in *New issues in the reconstruction of Shakespeare's theatre* (ed F J Hildy), New York, 55–78

Braines, W W, 1924 *The site of the Globe playhouse, Southwark*

Britton, F, 1987 *London delftware*

Brownstein, O, 1969 'The popularity of baiting in England before 1600: a study in social and theatrical history', *Educ Theat J* 21, 237–50

Buckley, F, 1915 *Old English glasshouses*

Buckley, F, 1930 'Old London glasshouses, I: Southwark', *J Glass Tech* 14, 137–49

Burford, E J, 1993 *The Bishop's brothels* (1st pub 1976 as *Bawds and lodgings*)

Cameron, R D A & Redfern, M, 1976 *British land snails* (*Mollusca: Gastropoda*), The Linnean Society of London Synopses of the British Fauna 6

Carlin, M, 1996 *Medieval Southwark*

Cerasano, S, 1991 'The Master of the Bears in art and enterprise', *Medieval and Renaissance Drama in England* 5, 195–209

Cerasano, S, 1994 'Edward Alleyn: 1566–1626', in *Edward Alleyn: Elizabethan actor, Jacobean gentleman* (ed A Reid & R Maniura), 11–31

Chambers, E K, 1923 *The Elizabethan stage* (4 vols)

Chew, S & Pearce, J, 1999 'A pottery assemblage from a 17th-century revetted channel at 12–26 Magdalen Street, Southwark', *London Archaeol* 9, 22–9

Clutton-Brock, J, 1974 'The Buhen horse', *J Arch Science* 1, 89–100

Collier, J P, 1831 *The history of English dramatic poetry*

Collier, J P, 1841 *Memoirs of Edward Alleyn, founder of Dulwich College*

Cowan, C, 1999 *Rear of 27 Bankside, Bear Gardens, London SE1: an archaeological evaluation,* MoLAS, unpub

Cowell, M, 1988 'Appendix 4: neutron activation analysis', in J Pearce & A Vince, 181–6

Culpeper, N, 1653 *The complete herbal*

Dawson, G, 1999 'Southwark in Domesday Book', *Southwark & Lambeth Archaeol Soc Newsletter* 79, 4–5

Dawson, G E, 1964 'London's bull-baiting and bear-baiting arena in 1562', *Shakespeare Quarterly* 15, 97–101

Dennis, G & Hinton, P, 1983 'A medieval kiln group from Bankside, SE1', *London Archaeol* 4, 283–7

Draper, M (ed), 1952 *List of records of The Corporation of Wardens of St Saviour Southwark*

Driesch, A von den, 1976 'A guide to the measurement of animal bones from archaeological sites', *Peabody Museum Bull* 1

Driesch, A von den & Boessneck, J A, 1974 'Kritische ammerkungen zur widerristhöhenberechnung aus langenmassen vor-und frühgeschichtlicher tierknochen', *Säugetierkundliche Mitteilungen* 22, 325–48

Dyson, T, 1980 'London and Southwark in the seventh century and later', *Trans London Middlesex Archaeol Soc* 31, 83–95

Egan, G, in prep a 'Report on window glass from the site of Bermondsey Abbey'

Egan, G, in prep b 'Report on window glass from the site of Merton Priory'

Ellis, A E, 1969 *British snails – a guide to non-marine Gastropoda of Great Britain and Ireland: Pleistocene to recent*

Foakes, R A & Rickert, R T (eds), 1961 *Henslowe's diary*

Frank, S, 1982 *Glass and archaeology*

Gaimster, D, 1997 *German stoneware 1200–1900: archaeology and cultural history*

Gairdner, J & Brodie, R H, 1910 *Letters and papers foreign and domestic of the reign of Henry VIII,* vol 21, 2

Godfrey, E S, 1975 *The development of English glassmaking 1560–1640*

Graham, A H, 1978 'The geology of north Southwark and its topographical development in the post-Pleistocene period', *Southwark Excavations 1972–74,* 2, London Middlesex Archaeol Soc/Surrey Archaeol Collections, 501–17

Grant, A, 1975 'The animal bones', in *Excavations at Portchester castle* (ed B Cunliffe), vol 1: *Roman,* Soc Antiq London Research Committee Report 32, 378–408

Grant, A, 1982 'The use of toothwear as a guide to the age of domestic ungulates', in *Ageing and sexing animal bones from archaeological sites* (ed B Wilson, C Grigson & S Payne), BAR British ser 109, 91–108

Greg, W W (ed), 1904 *Henslowe's diary, part 1: Text*

Greg, W W (ed), 1907 *Henslowe papers, being documents supplementary to Henslowe's diary,* New York ed, 1975

Greg, W W (ed), 1908 *Henslowe's diary, part 2: Commentary*

Grieve, M, 1931 *A modern herbal,* 1994 ed

Hanf, M, 1983 *The arable weeds of Europe – with their seedlings and seeds,* Ludwigshafen, Germany

Harcourt, R A, 1974 'The dog in prehistoric and early historic Britain', *J Arch Science* 1, 151–75

Heard, K A, 1996 *Post-excavation assessment of the clay tobacco pipes from an evaluation at Benbow House, Bear Gardens, Southwark, SE1,* MoLAS Archive Report

Henkes, H, 1994 *Glas zonder Glans,* Rotterdam Papers 9, Rotterdam, Netherlands

Hinton, M, 1980 'Medieval pottery from a kiln site at Kingston upon Thames', *London Archaeol* 3, 377–83

Janus, H, 1982 ed *The illustrated guide to molluscs*

Jones, M, 1988 'The arable field: a botanical battleground', in *Archaeology and the flora of the British Isles* (ed M Jones), 86–92

Kenward, H K & Hall, A R, 1995 'Biological evidence from Anglo-Scandinavian deposits at 16–22 Coppergate', in *The archaeology of York, vol 14: The past environment of York* (ed P V Addyman)

Kerney, M, 1999 *Atlas of the land and freshwater molluscs of Britain and Ireland*

Kingsford, C L (ed), 1908 *A survey of London by John Stowe* (2 vols)

Kingsford, C L, 1920 'Paris Garden and the bear-baiting', *Archaeologia* 70, 155–78

Le Cheminant, R, 1981 'Armorials from Paul's Wharf', in *The archaeology of the clay tobacco pipe, 6: Pipes and kilns in the London region* (ed P Davey), BAR British ser 97

Macan, T T, 1977 *A key to the British fresh- and brackish-water gastropods,* Freshwater Biological Association

McDonnell, K, 1978 *Medieval London suburbs*

Markham, G, 1633 *Country contentments: or, the husbandmans recreations*

Miller, P & Stephenson, R, 1999 *A 14th-century pottery site in Kingston upon Thames, Surrey: excavations at 70–76 Eden Street,* MoLAS Archaeology Studies ser 1

Morris, J (ed), 1975 *Domesday Book, 3: Surrey*

Noël Hume, I, 1995 'All aboard at Jamestown', *Colonial Williamsburg* 17.4, 22–33 (US)

Orton, C R, 1998 'Post-Roman pottery', in *Excavations in Southwark 1973–76, Lambeth 1973–79* (ed P Hinton), London Middlesex Archaeol Soc/Surrey Archaeol Soc, joint pub 3, 295–364

Oswald, A, 1975 *Clay pipes for the archaeologist,* BAR 14

Pearce, A, 1929 *The history of the Butchers' Company*

Pearce, J, 1992 'Border wares', in *Post-medieval pottery in London, 1500–1700,* vol 1

Pearce, J & Vince, A, 1988 *A dated type-series of London medieval pottery, part 4: Surrey Whitewares,* London Middlesex Archaeol Soc Special Paper 10

Pipe, A & Cowie, R, 1998 'A late medieval and Tudor horse burial ground: excavations at Elverton Street, Westminster', *Arch J* 155, 226–51

Planning Policy Guidance 16 (PPG 16), 1990 *Archaeology and planning*

Rackham, D J, 1995a 'Physical remains of medieval horses', in *The medieval horse and its equipment* (ed John Clark), 19–22

Rackham, D J, 1995b 'Appendix: skeletal evidence of medieval horses from London sites', in *The medieval horse and its equipment* (ed John Clark), 169–74

Rendle, W, 1878 *Old Southwark and its people*

Rielly, K, in prep *The animal bones from Vinegar Yard, Southwark,* Environmental Archaeology Section, Museum of London Specialist Services

Riley, H T (ed), 1868 *Memorials of London life in the XIIIth, XIVth and XVth centuries, A.D. 1276–1419*

Saxby, D, 1996 *Benbow House, Bear Gardens, Bankside SE1: an archaeological evaluation,* MoLAS, unpub

Schmid, E, 1972 *Atlas of animal bones*

Southwark, 1995 *Unitary development plan*

Stace, C, 1991 *New flora of the British Isles*

Survey of London, 1950, vol 22: *Bankside. (The Parishes of St Saviour and Christchurch Southwark)*

Thompson, A, Westman, A & Dyson, T (eds), 1998 *Archaeology in Greater London 1965–1990: a guide to records of excavations by the Museum of London,* MoL Archaeological Gazetteer ser 2

Ward Perkins, J B, 1940 *London Museum medieval catalogue*

Watts, D C, 1990 'Why George Ravenscroft introduced lead oxide into crystal glass', *J Glass Tech* 31, 208–12

Watts, D C, 1993 'Identifying the glasshouses operating on the South Bank of the River Thames in the 17th to 19th centuries', *J Glass Tech* 34, 83–4

Watts, D C, 1995, 'A history of English glassmaking on the Thames south bank 3', *Glass Circle News* 62, 2–3

Wheeler, E, 1979 *The tidal Thames*

Wilson, C A, 1973 *Food and drink in Britain from the Stone Age to recent times*

INDEX

Compiled by Susanne Atkin

Page numbers in bold refer to illustrations.